JAN 1 2 2004

THE SWEDISH HOUSE

THE SWEDISH HOUSE

Photography by Ingalill Snitt • Text by Lars Sjöberg

THE MONACELLI PRESS

Contents

Silent Houses 8

Sörby 30

Seventeenth Century: The European Swede 46

Salaholm 68

Eighteenth Century: Enlightenment, Beauty, and Comfort 80

Nineteenth Century: Non-Aristocratic Mansion Builders 142

Toward a New Age 170

Nordic Wood Churches 186

Nordic Wood Towns 202

Silent Houses

Old, deserted houses are intriguing. Who lived there and what was their fate? Is the house "original" or has it been rebuilt or extended throughout the centuries? Could the house be restored, lived in?

A large number of older Swedish houses are waiting to be reborn, particularly those in remote locations far from main roads. These houses are perfectly situated for anyone seeking seclusion and unspoiled nature.

Such "silent houses" bear witness to large migrations from rural districts and small industrial areas, generally in the north, to the big cities, generally in the south. But it is not unreasonable to imagine that certain people will choose to live in smaller communities if there is a functioning infrastructure. More and more people may discover that a search for lasting values will, of necessity, take them away from big cities.

For centuries, European thinkers and philosophers have formulated opinions on utopian life, concerning not only lifestyle and social habits but also building. Indeed, an imagined ideal society has influenced the planning of towns and industrial communities ever since the Renaissance.

The iron foundry, an important factor in Swedish society, came into being in the seventeenth century. The De Geer family was one of the most famous manufacturers, producing iron on a large scale and owning foundries in Finspång, in the province of Östergötland, and Leufsta, in northern Uppland. Although many of the foundry owners were aristocrats, manufacturers did not fit into the old class society—the foundry owners could almost be seen as a new class. The iron foundries accounted for the majority of Sweden's foreign exports, yet they were situated in places far from the towns and agricultural centers. The ironworks and foundries developed into centers that came to be self-sufficient societies with their own social structures.

Opposite: Farmhouse in the parish of Nordingrå, Ångermanland. During the first half of the nineteenth century, the house was decorated with an impressive portico, reflecting how Gustavian design elements were modified by the rural Swedish population. The house is typical of the local "cross-building" tradition (a four-room layout). One of the four rooms is an entrance hall with a stairway to the upper floor.

Page 2: The weather-beaten facade of a centuries-old wood house.

Page 4: Stepladder and Gustavian corner cupboard at Ekensberg mansion in Södermanland.

Pages 6–7: Logs floating down the Klar River.

Above: Farmhouse at Ullånger in Ångermanland. The paneling is painted white, and the window frames have a rich architectonic design.

Opposite: Detail of the house in Nordingrå parish. The paneled timber frame was previously painted with red oxide. Windows with six large panes, as on the ground floor, were introduced to Sweden in the eighteenth century but were not commonly used until the nineteenth century.

Situated in the marshy backwoods of Uppland, the community associated with the Leufsta foundry was one of the first to give architectural expression to this new social structure. The mansion house is situated in the center, with a church, foundry store, school, and medical facilities for the foundry workers nearby. Villages of this kind have stood bereft of almost all life and industry since the beginning of the twentieth century. Most of the houses are still inhabited, but iron production has long since ceased. These centuries-old houses provide historical documentation of buildings of the highest quality.

Travels to Italy and the discovery of classical monuments during the eighteenth century provided a rich source of inspiration for northern Europeans; they soon tried to reproduce classical ideas in both their houses and gardens. A journey back in time to take a look at Scandinavian architecture might today provide similar inspiration. The centuries of practical experience developed by carpenters and joiners could be used to renovate abandoned houses.

New surfaces on old buildings—facades, roofing, or woodwork—always present a challenge. It is possible that invaluable cultural and historic worth have been lost during such "renovation" work. But for the experienced observer, such latter-day improvements are not a great problem. For example, too many older houses have had their windows replaced by modern standardized windows. Yet old photographs often hold the secrets to their original appearance. The biggest challenge is probably posed by houses that have endured many phases of alteration throughout the centuries. For the most part, it is sufficient to peel away the last fifty or hundred years of "improvements" to restore to the house its old identity.

It is the fashion in the early twenty-first century, particularly among affluent businesspeople, to buy and restore old mansion houses. Sometimes the results have been good, sometimes less so. Some structures have even been converted into modern conference centers; these reveal a particularly insensitive handling of Sweden's cultural heritage.

Opposite: Pediments and window lintels supported by corbels were elements of the neoclassical style, typical in Västernorrland from the mid-1800s on.

Overleaf: Farmhouse in the parish of Bjärtrå, Ångermanland. Design elements from townhouses built of stone in the mid-nineteenth century made their way into rural facades.

The importance of preserving traditional craft skills has been unquestioned for decades. This has undoubtedly led more and more people to appreciate old houses on their own merits, instead of simply as a framework for contemporary design trends.

The houses that now stand deserted and unused can be generally divided into two groups. First, there are the buildings from old rural society—dwellings on farm estates that stood beside cultivated fields, a tradition that stretches back almost into prehistory. These are the leftovers—the houses ignored when farms merged or a modern farmhouse was built next to an old one. Some were eventually transformed into storehouses, garages, and so on. Yet to the discerning eye, the old window frames and other fittings are still evident. It was only during the nineteenth century that two-story wood houses began to be built in the countryside. They can be seen mainly in the regions of Hälsingland and Ångermanland. Ostentatious displays of wealth, the upper stories of many of these houses were built for show only and were never furnished. The houses were constructed with horizontal timbers, often covered with board and batten paneling. Besides the traditional red-oxide paint, first white or yellow washes and later linseed-oil paints were used.

The second group of deserted buildings consists of remnants of nineteenth-century industrialization and of villages that grew up along the railroads. These new communities were expansive construction sites that included commercial buildings, schools, assembly rooms, and chapels. Some of these villages have gradually developed into modern towns—if "modern" means towns, mostly of brick and stone, built mainly after World War II when wooden, decorated, turn-of-the-century buildings began to be demolished. Deplorable examples of this can be found at Ljungby in Småland or Kramfors in Ångermanland.

Opposite: The Swedish Evangelical Mission church at Bollstabruk, built around 1900, is an example of the rich wood architecture that flourished during the late 1800s and early 1900s. Contemporary fondness for staircase turrets, verandas, fretwork, and the like created a lively exterior.

Overleaf: Interior of a house built during the mid-1800s with a horizontal timber frame and clay-plastered walls. The walls were marbleized up to the windowsills; the upper walls were covered with stenciled or printed paper. Handcrafted tile stoves with green, yellow, or brown glazes still dominated during the mid-1800s; from the 1860s on, factory-manufactured white tile stoves became more common.

Above: Landscape in the region of Dalarna, framed by bound-osier fencing.

Opposite: Detail of the facade of a farmhouse in the parish of Bjärtrå, Ångermanland. The house was built in the mid-1800s with paneled horizontal timbers.

Overleaf: Farmhouse in the parish of Bjärtrå, built during the mid-1800s. The entry piece was added in the early 1900s, when it was fashionable to add a porch with fretwork decorations to the front farmhouse door.

Other villages, such as Bollstabruk by the Ångerman River, have lost their role as transport or industrial centers, but their turn-of-the-century houses are in danger nonetheless. One such example is the church that was built by the Swedish Evangelical Mission around 1900. Its original function is obsolete, and the building is now threatened with demolition.

In certain areas it has been customary not to tear down an old house when a new one was built nearby, probably for both sentimental and economic reasons. This is particularly true in northern regions such as Hälsingland and Ångermanland. These "silent houses" are biding their time, waiting only for new inhabitants with a genuine interest in tradition. One house in particular, in Ullånger in the High Coast district of Ångermanland, will soon be reborn. Its architectural integrity is being restored in a process that often requires the use of old carpentry methods to preserve the original joinery.

Sadly, a large number of horizontal-timber houses were demolished and used as firewood during the freezing winters of World War II. Large country houses that were considered too large to keep warm met a similar fate, as did many other large houses, particularly those rebuilt or extended during the nineteenth century.

The Torpa country mansion in Västergötland, for example, met such a fate. It was a horizontal-timber building constructed during the second half of the seventeenth century; a second story was added at the beginning of the nineteenth century. During demolition, a painted baroque ceiling was discovered under the later layers of fabric and board.

Two wooden seventeenth-century wings of Sjöholm mansion outside Katrineholm were also demolished, apparently when one of the wings was altered during the nineteenth century to serve as the main building after an older *corps de logi* (main building) had burned. The buildings at Torpa and Sjöholm are depicted in Erik Dahlberg's set of engravings *Suecia antiqua et hodierna* (c. 1700). These cultural jewels were replaced in both instances by new suburban housing.

Opposite: Exterior windows and doors often reveal the interior layout of the house. The entrance hall of this two-story house, with its richly decorated doorway, is lit by half-windows on either side of the front door. This indicates that the house has a six-room design, stemming from the Swedish manor-house tradition.

Overleaf: Swedish rural farmsteads and villages were a clutter of unpainted wood houses. In the village of Norrboda in Dalarna, the houses remain untouched by red-oxide paint, keeping alive a centuries-old building tradition.

Above: Covered entrance to an enclosed farmstead with unpainted timber facades at Norrboda in Dalarna. This farmstead displays the building traditions that prevailed before red-oxide paint and separate farmhouses became common during the first half of the nineteenth century.

Opposite: Weathered by sun and wind, this gray wall, made of round-edged timbers, reflects an early medieval tradition.

Sörby

The Sörby estate lies in the parish of Mosjö in Närke. The remaining mansion can be reliably dated back to the second half of the seventeenth century. The height of the building was increased somewhat during the mid-1700s, and new, larger window frames were installed. But the structure retains its original layout and proportions, except for two small rooms in the east wing that were combined into one during the Gustavian period (c. 1780).

The measurements of the house are carefully recorded in fire insurance documents of 1782. Measured in the then contemporary units of ell and inch (one ell is equal to 45 inches, or about 1.14 meters), the house was 20 ell 14 inches long, 12 ell 23 inches wide, and 7 ells high. It was constructed with both new and used timber and had a "good bark and turf roof" according to the insurance document. The windows of that time were nearly square, 1 ell 20 inches high by 1 ell 19 inches wide. When the nineteenth-century exterior paneling was removed, traces of the lower and wider seventeenth-century windows were found.

By studying the changes to the Sörby house, it is possible to discern certain general characteristics. The present appearance of the building might be regarded as original, but it has, in fact, undergone a gradual evolution. For example, in 1821, when the fire insurance was renewed, the windows had "leaded, white glass," which had presumably been installed in 1763 during a thorough renovation. The turf roof, laid on birch bark, had been replaced with tiles, and for the first time it is noted that the facade is painted with red-oxide paint. Though neither the original windows nor the roof remain, paintings on woven cloth, hidden behind the wallpaper in five ground-floor rooms, have survived.

These paintings derive from a new owner, Erik Waller, a vicar from Örebro, who wished to have his house insured in 1782. A preacher and also a couturier, he had come into contact with Stockholm culture and the royal court. This atmosphere was without question the inspiration for the artistic wall decorations at Sörby. As couturier, Waller had created the so-called national costume as the winner of a competition organized by the Royal Patriotic Society. His career

Opposite: An empty niche, which once housed a tile stove, in the drawing room at Sörby. This room was previously divided into two smaller rooms; the Gustavian wall painting is preserved only in one of the rooms.

Overleaf: During the Gustavian period, the upper walls of the drawing room at Sörby were covered with white linen painted with hanging garlands of flowers. The original small-paned windows were replaced during the 1850s.

was crowned by his appointment as bishop. He had a keen pedagogical interest in schools and the improvement of education. It is possible he purchased the house at Sörby as a symbol of his achievements.

Unlike most of the country mansions depicted in Erik Dahlberg's *Suecia antiqua et hodierna*, Sörby has timber walls right up to the roof ridge at the gable ends, which allowed for the installation of gable rooms at both ends of the attic. This specification is also stipulated in Stockholm town architect Johan Eberhard Carlberg's standard designs for officers' housing, as portrayed in engravings from 1731, in which the so-called manor roof was required. Carlberg also included suggestions for interior doors, window proportions, and fireproof hearths.

Sörby is in other ways very similar to Carlberg's army housing. Military rank was reflected in the size of the buildings, even though the characteristic two-part manor roof is integral to houses for both lieutenants and colonels. The "double-room" design, established in Dahlberg's 1687 plan for officers' dwellings, was replaced by the six-room design of 1731 (for captain, major, lieutenant colonel, and brigadier). This layout, which has its roots in Renaissance Italy, was introduced into Sweden during the early 1600s, though it was not brought into common use until the latter half of the century. The initial date of Sörby's construction is unknown. But since the Mannerberg family, owners of the house for three generations, declined at the beginning of the eighteenth century, the most likely construction period is 1660–1700.

The six-room design, which interlinks outer and inner walls, places the main entrance on the center axis. Typically, half windows on either side of the door light the entrance hall. The stairway to the attic is on one side of the central hall door, directly opposite the entrance. Doors leading to the gable rooms are on both ends of the hall. In the drawing room behind the hall or vestibule, similar doors lead to back rooms that have windows looking out to the garden.

According to the designs of 1730–31 drawn up by Carlberg, ground-floor rooms are heated by large open hearths. The hearth in one of the gable rooms is designed as kitchen range, which suggests that this room might have been used for preparing food, even though there was probably a separate building for

Above: Elevations of doors for officers' housing from 1731 by Johan Eberhard Carlberg. The two types of doors reflect different rankings.

Opposite: This section view shows a one-story timbered house with a saddle roof and a gable room in the attic.

Sch.

Profil utaf Öfwerste Bostelletz Caracter

Bygnad warandes Öfwerste Lieutnantz Caracter bygnad af lika profil.

Understa wåningen ifrån A till B eller emel-
lan gålfwet och bielkarne, blifwer 5 alnar hög, och
bräderne i panelningen   lägges under bielkarne.
ifrån B till C år 11 quar.   ifrån C til D 7 quar.

Regiments Qvartermästare och Cornets samt

Gafwelen

Framsidan

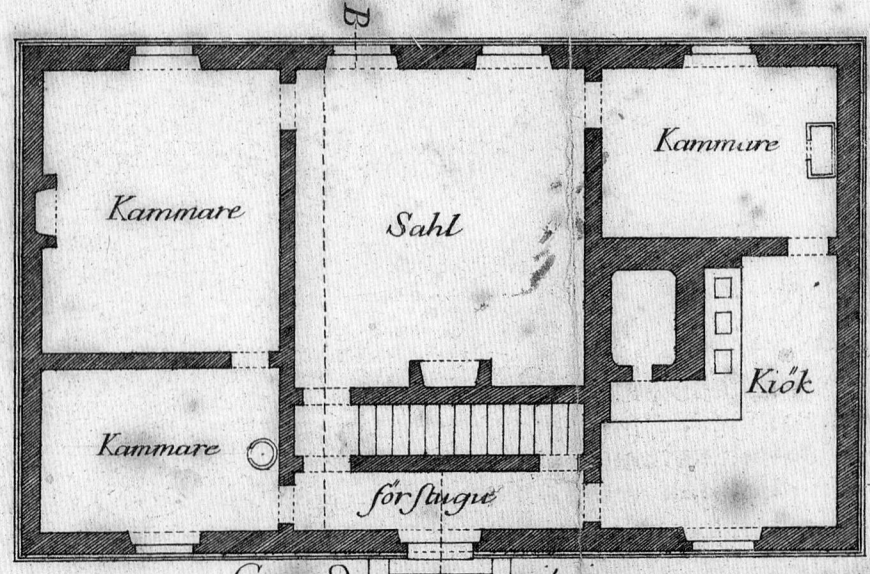

Grund-ritning

Lieutnants och Fändrichs Boställe

cooking. The room could not have been used for baking since there is no oven. The woodwork and plaster ceilings at Sörby probably date from 1760–80. The present interior doors are not those described in the 1782 fire insurance documentation. These were plain doors with four vertical panels of similar size—a design used by Nicodemus Tessin the Elder as early as the seventeenth century. The present doors are so-called half-French paneled doors, with three stacked panels. This type of door was a result of architect Carl Hårleman's efforts to introduce modern, French-inspired joinery into Sweden. Hårleman himself preferred the "whole-French" door, which has different moldings around the panels.

Hårleman also introduced the idea of a dado reaching up to the level of the windowsill or seat. A simple dado consisted of horizontal, planed planks topped with a dado rail. The Swedish baroque period saw the introduction of paneling in window recesses, but the walls in general had a lower skirting board. During the late eighteenth century, the paneling was raised to meet the bottom of the window. The dado could also consist of framed panels around all walls, as well as window recesses, in houses with plastered walls.

At Sörby, framed paneling appears only beneath the windows. The walls are treated with horizontal-plank paneling topped with a strip of braiding. This braiding was usually used to affix a wall covering of either textile, paper, or painted linen. The top of the wall covering was attached under the cornices and its sides to the windows or doors.

Former traditions manifest themselves not only in leaded windows but also in door proportions. Doors in old timber houses were generally wide and low. The usual Vasa Renaissance (named after Gustavus Vasa, who became King Gustavus I in 1523) doors had two similar panels, usually placed to one side (except doors made of planks). The door frames at Sörby are probably older, with the half-French doors themselves added later, sized to fit into the baroque frames. They are not more than 180 centimeters high.

One possible reason doors were not taller was that older timber houses had thresholds, not only to reduce drafts but also as inherent elements of construction. The threshold was created by the foundation log between the inner and outer walls, which held the framework together. When thresholds are lowered in old houses the result is often a loss of "tightness" in the whole building.

Opposite: A design for officers' housing by Carl Hårleman, around 1750. The engravings are by Jean Eric Rehn. The house has a six-room plan and a mansard roof, similar to other designs by Hårleman. It was intended to be a masonry building.

The price of glass usually dictated short windows—the smaller the windows, the cheaper they were. But short windows did not let in much daylight. And considering that green or discolored glass was cheaper than so-called white (transparent) glass, poorer people lived in rather dark interiors. Tall windows, on the other hand, required a better timber framework with superior construction. Large windows were also a source of heat loss, which meant that window size was also a factor in thermal economy. For all these reasons it is not difficult to understand why most houses had low ceilings until the eighteenth century. Ceilings of rural houses in the province of Östergötland, for example, were barely six feet high.

Introduced in 1767, the tile stove, with its system of heating channels, was a major invention of the eighteenth century. Though its use was initially slow to spread, it came to revolutionize living conditions in a way that can scarcely be imagined. It was presumably the tile stove that created the possibility for larger windows, higher ceilings, and all-year living in more of the available rooms.

The construction and design at Sörby represent an architectural tradition that percolated down through the classes and is reflected in countless houses built during the eighteenth and nineteenth centuries in different parts of the country. One example of this is the inn at Bratteberg in the parish of Regna, Östergötland, where two wings were added during the 1850s. The layout, measurements, and proportions are almost identical to those of the seventeenth-century building at Sörby. Bratteberg demonstrates how local owners added wings to their houses, just as the aristocracy had done two hundred years earlier. The red-oxide-painted timbers and the window distribution are very similar to Sörby. The main differences are the larger and taller nineteenth-century windows and the roof. At Bratteberg, a saddle roof permits light into the attic. Both houses, on the other hand, have rooms at the gable ends, since their timber walls go right up to the roof ridge, in accordance with Johan Eberhard Carlberg's designs.

Above: Sörby before renovation. Shortly after the legal partition of the estate in the 1860s, a three-room extension was added. The facades were covered with horizontal and vertical board-and-batten paneling.

Opposite: Despite long periods of roof leakage and a collapsed ceiling, the Gustavian walls have been preserved in all but one room. The windows on the south facade had been enlarged; the lampblack-gray dado reveals the original height of the windowsills. The half-French paneled doors were installed in the 1780s when the rooms on the ground floor were furnished in the Gustavian style. The wall coverings are decorated with hanging bay-leaf laurels.

Reawakening a Silent House

I first became aware of Sörby in 1988. It was not in good condition, but the house had an interesting history. The building had stood empty for a decade. Its exterior was typical of many estate buildings from the mid- and late nineteenth century. Tall trees, bushes, and wild undergrowth had enveloped the house, filling the gutters with decaying leaves that had caused rotting in the roof trusses, joists, and framework. Parts of the roof and rafters had fallen in; the sky was visible from the bottom floor, two stories below. The boarded-up windows had not prevented "treasure seekers" from searching through mattresses and featherbeds following the death of the extremely tight-fisted squire and the move of his elderly housekeeper. (The unmarried squire died without heirs, and his faithful servant, who lived to 106, inherited nothing.)

But dark, late-nineteenth-century wallpaper, collapsed ceilings, and rotting floors could not conceal the underlying older house with its eighteenth-century furnishings. The extensions were nineteenth-century in character. In three of the four older rooms, small remains of eighteenth-century painted-linen wall coverings could be found. The fourth room was a kitchen that contained a covered cooking hearth and a built-in bench beneath a plate rack. The older, six-room, horizontal-timber house could be quite easily discerned, despite the large extension along the length of the house and an added second floor in the central part.

The six-room design, or "mansion house plan," consisted of six rooms, including the hallway. The drawing room lay right behind the entrance and hallway, with two outward-facing rooms on each side. The so-called gable rooms were bedrooms. The kitchen was originally in an adjacent building. The six-room plan was introduced in the seventeenth century in smaller timber mansion houses, replacing the older and more primitive "double-room" plan, simply two similarly sized rooms on each side of an entrance hall.

With the assistance of an assiduous local craft historian, who had long studied his ancestral village, I discovered that the farmstead had originally been a

Above: Sörby after renovation. The board-and-batten paneling was removed, revealing the original timber framework of the main building. The larger windows of the entrance hall were reconstructed and restored to their former position. The original roof, lost during nineteenth-century extension work, was reconstructed according to Carlberg's plans for officers' housing and covered with tarred-wood shingles.

Opposite: The sawed-off timbers of the gabled east facade indicate the original placement of the attic room, in accordance with Carlberg's designs.

mansion or manor house held in aristocratic ownership during the seventeenth century. The family had crested graves in the parish church.

The former status of the mansion house was retained and strengthened when Sörby was divided by legal partition in the nineteenth century. Of the old village, where seven or eight close-built cottages had once stood, only the parish vicarage and the former manor farm were left.

The residence at the vicarage had been rebuilt after a fire in the second half of the nineteenth century. Thus, of all the houses in the parish, only the mansion house itself helps to document late-seventeenth-century building techniques.

The old house was owned by the State Forestry Commission, at Jönköping, which seemed interested neither in selling nor in partitioning the house. The estimate for renovation was deemed unacceptably high, and therefore the commission had decided on demolition. The Örebro Museum had been offered all furnishings of any worth. My interest in purchasing and preserving the building became known to the museum just as wall coverings from one of the decorated rooms were being cut out. The decision to demolish was canceled; the wall coverings were restored to the house when the sale was completed in 1988–89.

I wondered whether I should restore the house in its 1860s form or demolish the extension and return the house to its original condition. First, I had to examine the possibility of preserving the nineteenth-century exterior, but finding a carpenter or building contractor to repair the house, with its quasi-faulty construction, proved to be impossible. The house could not be preserved in its nineteenth-century condition because during the extension work, the timber walls of the upper story had been built directly on the lower story, without foundations. This was also true of the chimney. Moreover, the roof construction was botched. My project became, quite simply, a matter of removing the part of the building that had been "hung on."

After a preliminary roof repair, to prevent further destruction, an unexpected solution arose. During the early 1990s, a critical scrutiny of developments in the building sector concerning "sick" houses and poor materials had begun in Sweden. The State Building Society was attempting to regain both aesthetics and durability in housing. Public debates were initiated on the relevance of eighteenth-century designs and materials to modern functional demands. Researchers, contractors, and architects expounded the advantages of the six-room design (as at Sörby) and self-ventilation, or the exchange of air through fireplaces and chimney flues.

Opposite: Sörby before renovation. The attic room in the added upper story has larger-paned windows from the 1860s.

In 1989, recently revealed wall decorations from the drawing room at Sörby were shown in Paris during the two-hundredth anniversary of the French Revolution, and in 1990, Sörby was part of an exhibition at the Kortka Museum in Finland in connection with the anniversary of the 1790 battle at Svensksund. At the Kortka Museum, one of the rooms from Sörby mansion, showing samples of eighteenth-century wallpaper, flooring, walls, paneling, doors, and a tile stove, was reconstructed.

What finally decided Sörby's fate was an exhibition in Stockholm. The State Building Society and the National Museum had decided to erect a reproduction of Sörby for exhibition next to the National Museum in Stockholm. The building contractor for this project had to take down the nineteenth-century extension at Sörby in order to obtain timber for the reconstruction in Stockholm. Thus, only the old manor house framework was left, which was then covered with a new roof according to the original design. Subsequently, the roof has been laid with tarred shingles and the chimneys rebuilt. The enlarged, nineteenth-century windows of the south facade have been replaced with new frames that have casings made to the model of the eighteenth-century windows remaining on the east gable and north facade. A great deal of restoration work still remains to be done, including the replacement of flooring destroyed by mold and rot.

The external appearance of the house, now diminished to its original size, gives a good idea of a small late-seventeenth- or early-eighteenth-century Swedish mansion. Such buildings served as a model for Swedish army officers' housing. In principle, Sörby is identical with the 1730–31 prototype designs for officers' houses throughout Sweden, which feature a two-part manor roof, two symmetrically placed chimneys, and red-oxide-painted timbers. Inspiration was drawn from Andrea Palladio's writings on symmetry and proportion. Palladio, one of the most influential sixteenth-century Italian architects, became best-known for his villas, in contrast to most of his contemporaries, who focused on public or sacred buildings. His ideas and work came to characterize houses in Sweden from the middle of the seventeenth century on.

The Palladian villas erected on Italian estates were built with stone, but their clear designs and visual motifs could easily be translated into timber. The most characteristic features are symmetry and an accented center axis. In Swedish houses inspired by Palladio's designs, the largest room, usually the drawing room, is often centrally placed.

Opposite: Andrea Palladio's designs were published in his Four Books on Architecture. *The sixteenth-century woodcuts were disseminated as engravings in the seventeenth and eighteenth centuries.*

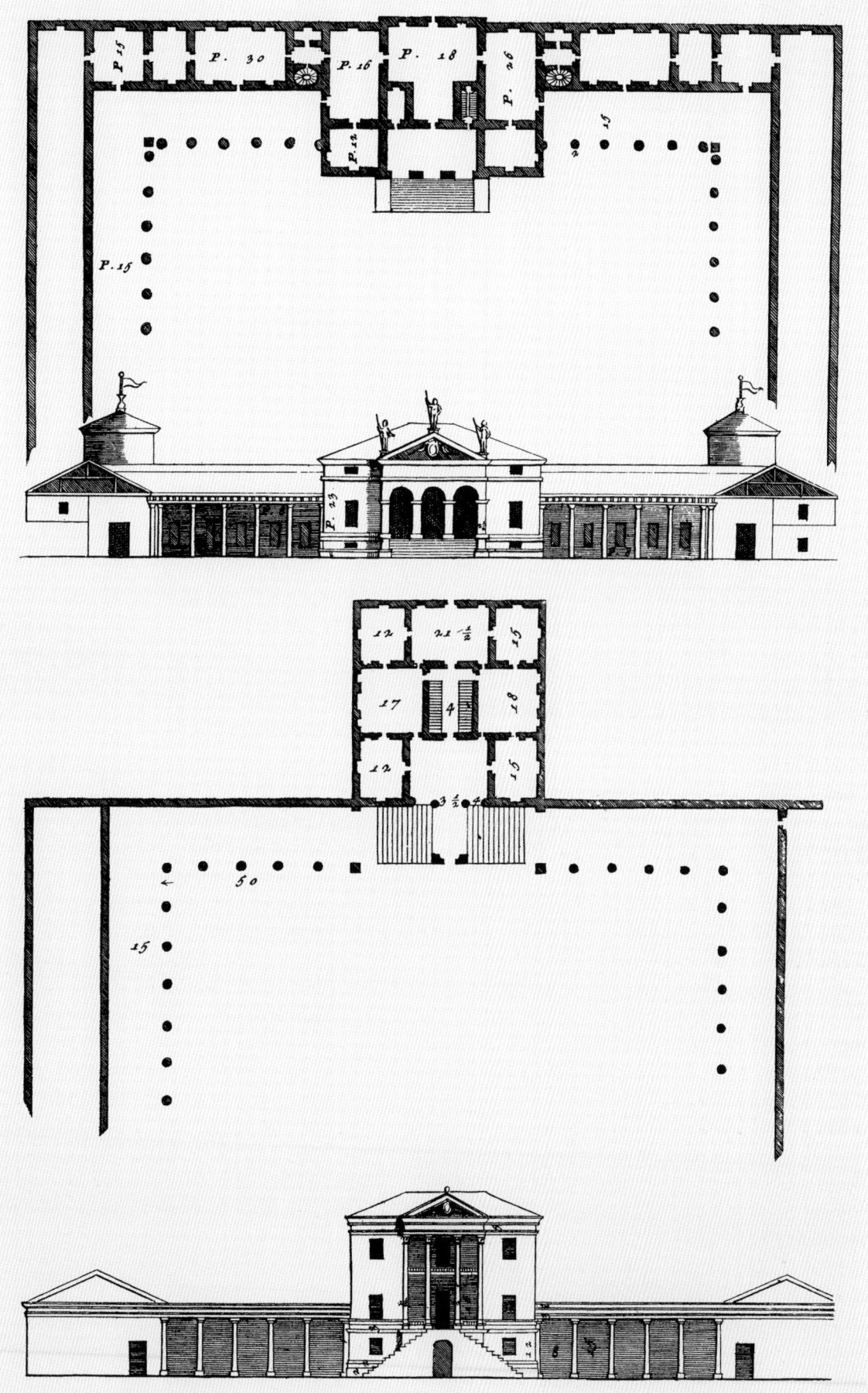

Seventeenth Century: The European Swede

A study of the so-called Tova cottage, currently sitting on the castle grounds at Nyköpingshus, helps explain the progress of the Swedish nobility from the early seventeenth century on. The main building comes from a manor in the district of Sörmländ and dates back to the early seventeenth century. The exterior resembles a modest double-room house, and the small windows and unpainted exterior walls hardly suggest distinguished elegance to the modern observer. But the reception room on one side of the entrance hall has a surprising monumentality. Its painted timber walls help create an impression of space and volume under the high rafters. On the outside, the turf roof reaches so far down that it is difficult to stand upright under the eaves.

Even though few early-seventeenth-century timber mansion houses similar to Tova cottage survive in their original form, rural buildings from the eighteenth century echo the same austere, almost primeval introspection. It appears as if nature itself has stipulated the color scheme.

Läckö Castle

Until the Thirty Years' War (1618–48), most Swedes, including the aristocracy, lived in medieval-style, unpainted, turf-roofed timber houses. Castles and royal fortresses had been built during the Middle Ages, such as those in Kalmar and Stockholm. Catholic bishops also built castles and fortified houses, which after the Reformation were transformed into crown fortresses or palaces or simply demolished.

One such bishop's stronghold was Läckö Castle on a promontory at Lake Vänern in Västergötland. The castle was founded in the thirteenth century for the bishop of Skara and extended until the fall of the Catholic Church in the 1520s, when Lutheran teaching was adopted in Sweden. King Gustav Vasa and the state subsequently took over church property. Läckö Castle and the king's estate there were lent to field marshal Jacob De la Gardie in 1615. Until 1680, when the crown again confiscated the castle, it was the center of an earldom that provided a cultural focus for two generations of sculptors and painters and had a court life with international ambitions.

Jacob De la Gardie and his son, Magnus Gabriel, span the period when Sweden was an imperial power. Jacob De la Gardie captured Moscow with Swedish troops in 1610 and also captured the town of Novgorod for Karl IX. (Jacob's father, Pontus, had in

Opposite: Aristocratic palaces during the seventeenth century reflected the desire to model Sweden on classical ideals. The baroque interior at Läckö Castle was created with planks, nails, and paint during the late 1600s.

Overleaf: The King's Hall at Läckö Castle. Stepped cupboards stand beneath two galleries, which are supported by pillars. The paintings on linen and wood reflect the skill of late-seventeenth-century painters and joiners.

the late 1500s incorporated Estonia into the Swedish empire.) Jacob had almost succeeded in making Karl IX's younger son, Karl Filip, the Russian czar. On his return from Russia, Jacob De la Gardie married Gustav II Adolf's teenage sweetheart, Countess Ebba Brahe. During the 1630s, he built the most magnificent private palace of the time, Makalös ("Incomparable") in Stockholm.

Previously, he had decorated the walls and ceilings of Läckö Castle with an antiquated, almost folkloric version of Renaissance art, derived from engravings. De la Gardie and Ebba Brahe built their first country house at Jacobsdal outside Stockholm. It was constructed with horizontal timbers and, according to the French ambassador at Stockholm, was reminiscent of the farmhouses around Paris. This prompted the former general to start building a stone edifice that was to form the core of the present-day palace at Ulriksdal, just north of Stockholm.

During the 1630s and 1640s—while the Thirty Years' War raged across the Baltic and the Swedish crown captured territory in north Germany—the need grew for prestigious buildings that would prove to the world that Sweden was indeed a land of high culture. Jacobsdal and Makalös were spectacular such constructions.

Jacob's son, Magnus Gabriel De la Gardie, had a fast-rising career, both military and civilian. He was ambassador in Paris at the age of twenty and, two years later, in 1648, participated in the storming of Prague. His taste for high European culture led him, throughout the rest of his life, to attempt to introduce some of this culture into Sweden. He initiated numerous construction projects and ornamentation programs.

At his father's death in 1652, Magnus Gabriel took over the earldom and Läckö Castle. During the next three decades, a large garden was planted, a chapel and new towers were added to the castle, and a fourth story was added to the old stronghold. The castle came to comprise more than two hundred rooms in wings around three courtyards. In 1680–81, when the crown confiscated a great deal of property from nobility, the castle was emptied of its furniture and the rooms have stood empty ever since. With the exception of a few rooms on the third floor, the seventeenth-century built-in furnishings remain almost intact.

Above: Läckö Castle dates from the thirteenth century but was enlarged and decorated by the De la Gardie family during the seventeenth century.

Opposite: Swedish folk traditions and classical ideals meet in the Geatish (Gothic-fantasy folklore style) drawing room.

Overleaf: This unfurnished room, known as His Majesty's Bedroom, was left unfurnished when the castle was taken over by the state in 1680.

Above: Evangelists carved in wood adorn the chapel built at Läckö Castle by Magnus Gabriel De la Gardie.

Opposite: Seventeenth-century plain wood floors remain in many rooms at Läckö Castle. The doors, on the third floor, have two elevated panels on one side and date from the mid-1600s.

Skokloster

It was not only Magnus Gabriel De la Gardie who felt the need to demonstrate his family's position in society. Other families who had lived in Sweden for a few generations, such as the Wrangels, demonstrated a strong desire to create monuments for posterity. They intended the "family fortresses" they built to compete with the mansion houses of older Swedish families.

During the 1630s, Herman Wrangel had contented himself with renovating a smaller stone house from a former monastery at Skokloster, in Uppland, characterized by high stepped gables and a virtual "double-cruciform" design. His son, Carl Gustaf Wrangel, began the construction of his own palace at Skokloster in 1654. (Strictly speaking, the term *palace* was reserved for royal property at that time.) It is almost a direct copy of the Polish Vasa family's summer residence outside Warsaw.

None of the monumentality and symmetry associated with the early seventeenth century was spared in the new palace. Skokloster had octagonal towers at each corner of a four-story quadrangle, with arcades around the inner courtyard. Lantern towers, one story higher, were crowned with cupolas, giving the whole building impressive height.

The exterior was completed in the 1660s. In terms of architectural innovation, Skokloster surpassed any royal palace in the country, with the exception of Borgholm Castle on the island of Öland. However, by the time of its completion, Skokloster was already old-fashioned, according to contemporary architectural taste, which favored Italian sixteenth-century villas. Andrea Palladio's country villas in northern Italy provided the model home for a new aristocratic lifestyle. A version of these country palaces was later developed in France and would influence the direction of the Swedish country estate.

Gripenberg

Carl Gustaf Wrangel also built timber palaces, three in all. Gripenberg Palace near Tranås in the parish of Säby in Småland survives with its baroque decoration intact and is probably the most expressive of Sweden's wood palaces. Work began during the winter

Opposite: The library at Skokloster. Exposed beams, plain wood floorboards, and painted wall swags were common in both wood and stone mansions in the seventeenth century. The furniture was usually simple and robust.

Overleaf: Gripenberg is one of the best-preserved wooden baroque palaces in Sweden. It was originally a red-oxide-painted timber building with a shingled roof. The facades were later painted yellow. The exterior is otherwise unchanged since Carl Gustaf Wrangel erected the palace in the 1650s and 1660s.

of 1663–64 but was still not finished at the time Skokloster was completed. The main building is a two-story H-shaped timber structure. At each corner are square, three-story towers with cupolas. Since the house was intended for hunting, only the ground floor was furnished. Carl Gustaf Wrangel visited his hunting palace only once, in 1669, two years after completion.

The outer walls were originally painted with red-oxide paint and had gray pilasters and moldings under the high tarred-shingle roof. Like so many other seventeenth- and early-eighteenth-century buildings, the facades at Gripenberg were later covered with vertical paneling and painted yellow. The four rooms in the attic have never been fully furnished—a trait shared by many houses of this imperial period when outward appearance was paramount.

The fondness for large houses with corner towers evident at Gripenberg became popular not only in Sweden but also in Finland, which was part of Sweden's empire at this time. Otherwise, in the late 1600s, long, narrow, rectangular buildings, without projections, were typical. But toward the end of the century, Palladian-style villas with projecting central drawing rooms were developed, similar to the stone mansions at Sjöö and Salsta. In any case, it was most important for mansion builders to create something imposing—high roofs, spires, a fully developed symmetry—in order to distinguish their houses from neighboring rural buildings.

Another convention for seventeenth-century mansion houses was a turret or lantern centered on the roof or a high hipped roof (the gable does not reach the roof ridge; the roof slopes on all four sides). Presumably, this new generation of builders was not satisfied with an imposing manor roof, that is, a two-part roof with timber walls up to the ridge, often with windows to allow light into the unfurnished attic.

Bordsjö

The Bordsjö estate in the parish of Askeryd, Småland, features a seventeenth-century, timber, one-story main building. Before its eighteenth-century renovation, the house had plain, red-oxide-painted timber walls. Its double drawing rooms recall Gripenberg. According to a contemporary description, Bordsjö had a rounded projection on each side of the entrance hall and a terrace with towers.

The two projections disappeared during an 1863 conversion, which also included the construction of the present-day roof with its central tower. Nonetheless, Bordsjö is a good example of how even relatively modest buildings could be given an impressive monumentality.

Opposite: The timber main building at Bordsjö. Although it was enlarged and modernized, the house has retained its seventeenth-century character. The facades were previously painted with red oxide.

Above: The entrance hall at Sandemar, in the district of Haninge, Södermanland, has a double staircase with balusters, emphasizing the ceremonial character of the room.

Opposite: Few houses display such exuberant Swedish baroque character as Sandemar. The main building has several wings, built during the late seventeenth century by Count Gabriel Falkenberg. The two-story main building features paintings done directly on the axe-smoothed timber walls, such as this wooded landscape in the entrance hall.

Skogaholm

The most famous seventeenth-century timber mansion house in Sweden and abroad is a one-story building from Skogaholm's ironworks and foundry in Närke. It has stood at Skansen in Stockholm since about 1930. The house has a high manor roof and was originally painted with red oxide. The facade was roughcast and painted with a yellow wash during the late 1700s. Roughcasting a timber frame or covering it with vertical paneling was very common toward the end of the eighteenth century, both for newly built and modernized houses.

When the building was dismantled and moved to Skansen, the timber framework was temporarily revealed. However, it was decided to maintain the Gustavian character of the house, typified by the taller windows and pillared front entrance. Nevertheless, the high manor roof with its centrally placed lantern is original, as is the tarred-wood roof shingling.

After its move to Skansen, two wings from Gullaskruv in Småland, both horizontally timbered, were added to Skogaholm. While the facades retained their red-painted timbers, the wings also have hipped manor roofs with tarred shingles. In a desire to re-create the baroque symmetry of the estate, two square pavilions were placed at the far end of the outer courtyard, a fashion that first emerged during the mid-1600s in both stone and timber mansions.

Mariedal

Mariedal in Västergötland is one of the oldest and best-documented estates of the mid-1600s. The building contractor was Magnus Gabriel De la Gardie, who initiated work on the site of the old Sörbo manor house for his wife, Princess Maria Eufrosyne.

Architect Jean de la Vallée designed the two-story main building. It is a rectangular structure with a high, hipped saddle roof crowned by a central lantern and spire. Two long, one-story wings were added later, with two square pavilions at the courtyard entrance.

Two timbered wings, with steep-roofed porches, framed the courtyard during De la Gardie's time. But a 1740 oil painting of the baroque estate portrays the new wings and pavilions, built in both stone and wood in an archaic Caroline style. All four early-eighteenth-century wings had two-level manor roofs, while the pavilion roofs were S-shaped. The new wings were constructed while De la Gardie was the owner.

Opposite: Skogaholm mansion was built in Närke and moved to Skansen in Stockholm. It was erected at the end of the seventeenth century, and its facade originally had red-oxide-painted horizontal timbers.

Sjöö

Another property belonging to Magnus Gabriel De la Gardie was Sjöö, in the parish of Holm, Uppland, which was built during the 1670s. The design for Sjöö—by Nicodemus Tessin the Elder—is a variation on one of Palladio's early villas from the 1540s. The on-site architect was Mathias Spieler, who presumably designed the eight symmetrically positioned wings and pavilions. The two wings joined to the main building were two-story stone buildings erected for Johan Gabriel Stenbock. They are sited with the main building on a higher terrace. Four buildings were erected around an outer courtyard in front of the terrace—two square gatehouses and two longer side wings. These four 1670s buildings were copied at Mariedal in Västergötland in the early eighteenth century.

Framing the outer courtyard of a mansion house with two square pavilions was an important baroque architectural device, on both larger and smaller estates. The pavilions often had tentlike or conical roofs, since the buildings were used as storehouses for grain, foodstuffs, or clothes. Smaller pavilions might have been used as pleasure houses or privies. Timbered, cubic, and austere, they stand on guard like defense towers for aristocratic mansions throughout Sweden.

Fårbo and Tubbetorp

Two of the granaries at Fårbo estate, on the Småland coast, have tarred roofs made of overlapping planks. The flanking storehouses on Tubbetorp estate near Skara in Västergötland have slate roofs. The effect of framing the courtyard is the same in both cases. The windowless walls painted with red oxide, the wide doors with their iron fittings convey an impression of lingering imperial power—a kind of rustic monumentality created with native materials. The scent of tar reinforces the impression of a long-lost past and proud architectural visions fashioned centuries ago. Using only axe, knife, and brush, skilled craftsmen once created almost eternal values from timber, red-oxide paint, and tar.

Above: Apelhäster in the parish of Alseda in Småland. Two small pavilions have pyramidal roofs, as do the storehouses at Tubbetorp and Fårbo.

Opposite: One of the storehouses at Fårbo in Småland. The roof is made of tarred overlapping planks.

Salaholm

Few old houses or mansions speak so strongly of abandonment as those on the former estate of Salaholm in the parish of Trävattna, twenty kilometers west of Falköping in Västergötland. In the early 1600s, a new estate was built there, a short distance from the old residence, the site of a medieval mansion. The area was surrounded by streams, which facilitated the creation of avenues of trees as well as a garden framed by moats.

The oldest surviving maps from the end of the seventeenth century show that the estate had ten houses. The present house is identical to the former south wing of the old main building. A similar building on the north side was demolished as recently as the 1920s. Only some vaulted cellars under a ramshackle roof remain on the site of the seventeenth-century main building, although in the nineteenth century a pleasure house or garden pavilion stood there, possibly incorporating the remains of the old house.

The old main building, which was elegantly furnished and still inhabited at the end of the eighteenth century, was dismantled and moved to Höverö estate, belonging to the Fock family, several kilometers from Salaholm. This aristocratic family needed a more distinguished residence. The removal of the old main building must have occurred sometime during the first half of the nineteenth century, at the time when Salaholm as a whole was demolished.

According to seventeenth-century designs, the former main building was a long, narrow, one-story, horizontal-timber building with a high roof and central tower—similar to the remaining wing. In fact, it was possibly this central part of the house that was left to form the garden pavilion that remained until the late nineteenth century.

Traces of the former greatness of the estate are still discernable on the approach. An avenue of trees leading up to the gates meets another avenue leading south to the parish church.

In the 1620s, Erik Haraldsson Soop moved the manor house from Sahletorp to the present site of Salaholm and gave the house its more impressive new

Opposite: Salaholm mansion in Västergötland. The Gustavian doors and doorway are from the early 1890s. A narrow horizontal window allows light into the hall.

Overleaf: Of Salaholm's houses only the south wing remains. It was probably built during the seventeenth century, though the present exterior dates from 1813 when it was painted with red oxide. The high roof with hipped gable ends allowed for attic rooms at each end. The roof was originally covered with tarred shingles, although these were replaced by metal sheeting in the 1850s and most recently by tiles.

name. His daughter, Ebba Eriksdotter Soop, married into the Gyllengrip family, who resided at Salaholm until the mid-1700s. The estate owned almost the whole parish, as well as its own chapel in the nearby church. During the 1750s, Salaholm estate comprised almost eight thousand acres. Division of the estate began in the first half of the nineteenth century, but it was not until the early twentieth century that Salaholm was fully partitioned and lost its status as a manor or estate. The well-kept orchard—with its own varieties of fruit, such as the Salaholm apple—fell into neglect.

The old barn burned down during the 1890s and was replaced with a new storehouse with double stone ramps up to the hayloft; the main building was demolished to provide stone for these ramps. The new barn in turn burned down in the 1980s, leaving only the stone ramp foundations.

The irreverent treatment of cultural heritage at Salaholm is shocking. Oaks and other deciduous trees were cut down during the 1960s, not only in the park but also in the surrounding pastureland, to make room for a coniferous plantation. It is still possible to see traces of the garden that was laid out during the early 1600s. Ditches or moats frame three sides of the rectangular garden. Avenues, hedges, and straight rows of fruit trees convey the impression of an older, methodical order. An octagonal limestone table, dating from the 1670s, sits in what was once the southern orchard, now an overgrown arbor. The foundations of the north wing can still be discerned, and a low rise marks the place of the former main building.

Salaholm is something of a find for those interested in the history of gardening. There is a great deal to discover here, even though much is obscured by overgrown bushes and underbrush. A memorial stone sits along the avenue from the west wing of the house toward the streams. The murmuring of the adjacent waterways suggests the reason for choosing this site as a place for contemplation four hundred years ago.

The Exterior

An 1830 fire insurance document details the appearance of Salaholm at that time. The main building was

Opposite: The staircase in the entrance hall of Salaholm mansion has wooden banisters that imitate ironwork. The lower part is paneled with vertical planks and splatter-painted in black and white on a lampblack-gray ground. All the walls in the entrance hall were probably painted in this manner.

Overleaf: The kitchen at Salaholm was installed in the 1870s. Hardwood cupboards were added during the twentieth century. The French-paneled door is now the outer door of an added kitchen entrance.

already gone, although the two wings are described. They were constructed with horizontal timbers and were already covered with red-oxide-painted paneling. In order to obtain a higher insurance value, the wings were characterized as being built in the early nineteenth century, although they were merely renovated at that time. There was no kitchen in the remaining wings in 1830, but there were tile stoves, two of which were recessed porcelain stoves that heated all the rooms.

Thus, the house now standing at Salaholm has functioned as the main building for two hundred years. The house is crowned by a high roof with hipped gable ends. The outer measurements are ten by twenty meters. The layout is somewhat irregular: the rooms on both sides of the entrance are symmetrically placed, unlike the suite of rooms on the southern side.

The outer walls were paneled, most recently during the 1870s when they were also painted yellow, and have white window frames and moldings. Tall and narrow windows, installed during a renovation, remain on the gables, although on some facades they have been replaced by small-paned windows with shorter and wider frames, reconstructed from remains of eighteenth-century windows. The high roof provided space for two furnishable attic rooms at either end of the house. During the 1870s, the middle section of the south facade was increased in height to two stories, allowing for three more windowed rooms in the attic. These changes did not beautify the house. Instead, the front facade feels much more monumental, even contemporary.

The Interior

The cultural and historical value of Salaholm is priceless. The long suite of rooms on the southern side boasts fine proportions. It is possible to stand at one end of the house and see room after room in a diminishing perspective as light plays over paneling, doorframes, and moldings. This house was once furnished with great artistic care and traditional craft skills.

Above all else, it is perhaps flooring that gives a house its soul. Some of Salaholm's floors have probably been replaced over the years, and they have numerous layers of varnish and polish. But under the surface are the old, plain, wood floorboards that, together with the reflected light from the whitewashed ceiling, create a living historic environment.

Above: The largest room on the bottom floor at Salaholm is the drawing room at the east end. A tile stove with blue rococo decoration lost its original mantelpiece during a twentieth-century remodeling.

Opposite: View from the center of Salaholm mansion. The doors with three panels and rococo moldings probably date from the mid-1700s.

Only a few examples of seventeenth-century furnishing remain. With its decorated doors, paneling, and ceilings, Sandemar in the province of Södermanland—erected for Count Gabriel Falkenberg—is probably the best preserved. Embellishments of a kind usually found on linen wall coverings were painted directly on the timber walls of Sandemar's entrance hall. Wall decoration varied through the centuries. Rolls of printed wallpaper were first introduced during the second half of the nineteenth century, providing a cheap and easy way redecorate a room. One of the many things to consider when assessing an old house that has been renovated is whether older linen or paper wall coverings remain under the new wallpaper. If they have been removed, it is probably better to paint the walls in a color that will highlight the moldings and proportions of the room.

This is what museum official N. F. Behrstål did when he acquired the remaining building at Salaholm in the 1970s, except for the walls of the largest drawing room, which he decorated in a Gustavian style. In the same room, he installed a tile stove from the attic. This stove dates from the late 1700s and consists of different types of blue-and-white tiles that originally came from two other stoves. The reconstructed stove, however, was not given a mantelpiece, which would have been obligatory for tile stoves of this period. But it does have a traditional wood base.

During the second half of the eighteenth century, the ground was laid for what could be called the "modern home." Open hearths had begun to be replaced by tile stoves, as at Salaholm. In the present dining room, the open limestone hearth has been restored (it was probably used as a garden embellishment after being dismantled during an earlier renovation). Salaholm did not possess Sandemar's interior elegance. If there ever was such grace at Salaholm, it must have been in the main building.

Elegant or not, every old house has its secrets. Discoveries can be made in the cellar, attic, outbuildings, or double flooring. In these places may be found anything from old wallpaper to dismantled tile stoves, or the remains of previous furnishing. There might even be splatter-distemper decoration on the bare walls of a staircase, such as at Salaholm, where under the peeling wallpaper in the entrance hall is splatter painting done in lampblack gray.

Indeed, it is perhaps these very empty houses that leave the most room for imagination. Those who love old houses harbor a dream of re-creating them as they once were, thereby also restoring something of their soul.

Opposite: An outbuilding at Salaholm, with its original red-oxide-painted exterior, has begun to grow green during decades of neglect.

Eighteenth Century: Enlightenment, Beauty, and Comfort

In 1719–21, at the end of the Great Northern War, the Russians burned down many country mansions, ironworks, and foundries along the coast to force Sweden into negotiating a peace. The mansion house, church, and foundry workers' dwellings of the Leufsta iron foundry in Uppland, for example, went up in smoke. The decision during the eighteenth century to rebuild these burned mansions in stone and brick instead of timber not only provided more fireproof housing but also allowed for more sophisticated styles and better methods of construction.

Until the mid-eighteenth century, high manor roofs were usually made of tarred-wood shingles. Thereafter, these elegant shingles were replaced by less flammable glazed or unglazed tiles or by metal sheeting. These roofs represent the meeting of new French architectural ideals and the still lingering baroque style from the 1730s.

A single building can be either a mixture or the sum of several centuries of building styles. Palace architect Carl Hårleman's first modern mansion, Thureholm, near Trosa in Södermanland, is an example of a stylistically mixed building. Created in the late 1720s, the high roof is reminiscent of the seventeenth century, but the yellow-and-white color scheme of the facades represents the new eighteenth-century taste.

The changes in country mansions were not reflected in houses belonging to the less affluent. The so-called barter society lived on in the countryside. Unpainted, horizontal-timber houses with turf roofs still dominated during the seventeenth and eighteenth centuries.

Architecturally, it is not always easy to distinguish between the seventeenth and eighteenth centuries. During the seventeenth century, Sweden was striving to gain a position in Europe, building so diligently that it almost seems the Scandinavian country took as its model ancient Rome. However, Sweden lost its imperial status in the first decades of the eighteenth century, during Karl XII's reign. Reconstruction was necessary after the Peace of 1721 (following the treaty signed between Russia and Sweden that ended the Great Northern War). A style developed that could best be described as Caroline baroque, although it had begun to emerge as early as the second half of the seventeenth century. Nicodemus Tessin the Younger, Jean de la Vallée, and Mathias Spieler were its most famous architects and were widely imitated in the 1720s and 1730s.

The East India Company had imported Oriental influences into Europe during the seventeenth century. Interest in Chinese culture had already created a

Opposite: English-inspired Windsor armchair and Gustavian pullout bed at Regnaholm mansion in Östergötland. The window frames are from the 1760s.

Overleaf: The Swedish rococo dining room on the upper floor at Regnaholm, from the 1760s.

vogue in interior design. The Trianon de Porcelain, a pavilion inspired by blue-and-white Chinese porcelain and erected by Louis XIV in the garden of Versailles, is one example.

Faience workshops, particularly in Holland, made pottery and china services with Oriental motifs. Chinese lacquerwork had reached Sweden by the early 1600s. Gustavus Adolphus II was given a magnificent lacquered trunk in 1616, which has stood in the royal bedchamber at Gripsholm Castle since the reign of Gustav III.

Tall, turn-of-the-century grandfather clocks, with chinoiserie on the case, reflect the strong Oriental interest in Europe. Initially, no distinctions were drawn between Indian, Chinese, and Japanese cultures. Everything the East India Company ships brought was exotic and therefore attractive. The Oriental aesthetic seemed to suit the times. It was not only Chinese furnishings and objets d'art that fascinated the Swedes, but also Chinese life in general.

The craze for the Far East, particularly China, blossomed after the Peace of 1721. A wall painting featuring motifs from imperial China can be found at Ekebyholm, north of Rimbo in Uppland, which was furnished by Arvid Bernhard Horn, statesman and former soldier of Karl XII. One of the buildings at Hårleman's Thureholm can be seen as a tribute to Chinese art and culture. Most of the furnishing consists of Chinese porcelain, with motifs from the "forbidden city of Peking" and everyday Chinese life.

One of the most pressing concerns during the eighteenth century was the improvement of agriculture, the economic base of the country. Several books were published at midcentury—some by the Scientific Academy—containing suggestions on how agriculture could be improved by following Chinese models. The primary focus was the optimum use of natural resources during peacetime.

A special science, known as physiography, developed. According to the physiocrats, Chinese philosophy would become the ideological base for a new kind of society. Young Crown Prince Gustav (later Gustav III) was persuaded to embrace physiocratic ideas by the Scheffer brothers, Ulrik and Carl Fredrik. They believed that humankind's profound dependence on the earth and on agriculture should also influence the planning of palace and estate lands.

Opposite: Fine Swedish cabinetmaking and furniture crafting underwent unprecedented development during the eighteenth century. This dining room chair with crest, oval back, and baluster splat is one of many variations of the so-called Swedish model.

Overleaf: The orangery at Regnaholm mansion reflects the great interest in horticulture in Sweden at the end of the eighteenth century.

Carl Linnaeus

It is not easy in the present day to distinguish the imperial period from the eighteenth century without focusing on specific people and what they represented. The architectural ambitions of Magnus Gabriel De la Gardie and Carl Gustaf Wrangel are far removed from those of Carl Linnaeus. Carl von Linné, as he was known after he was raised to the peerage, was one of the great men of the eighteenth century, famous not only in Sweden but internationally. His life, as reflected in his surviving houses and gardens, can be assessed in terms of both social mobility and architectural development.

Son of a prelate, Linnaeus was born in Råshult vicarage in the parish of Stenbrohult in southern Småland, not far from Älmhult. The house where Linnaeus spent his early years was later replaced. The new house—built for Carl's brother—is still in its original location. It is one of Sweden's most important buildings and has been a pilgrimage site for Linnaeus enthusiasts since the nineteenth century. Its birchbark and turf roof, six-room layout, timbered walls, and leaded windows all serve to recall an architectural ideal and period that seem very distant.

Later renovation work, which included reexposing interior walls and reducing window sizes, was done with the goal of restoring Råshult to its original condition. Even if such architecturally motivated changes may seem heavy-handed, they nevertheless provide a chance to experience a house from the upper ranks of 1740s society. Many lesser eighteenth-century country houses were in the same style as the buildings at Råshult.

The Wedding Cottage

By the early sixteenth century, four represented estates, or classes—nobility, priests, bourgeoisie, and peasants—had been established in national meetings, the embryo of Sweden's modern parliament. This division would last for more than three hundred years. There were differences not only between the four estates during the eighteenth century but also within them. The so-called commoner estates had made

Opposite: An older, Renaissance-decorated door reused in the "mountain mansion" of Sveden in Dalarna.

Previous pages: Sveden is most famous for Carl Linnaeus's 1739 wedding celebration. This building, then newly constructed, has stylistic features from the seventeenth century.

Overleaf: The reception room in the Wedding Cottage has doors installed by Johan Eberhard Carlberg in 1731; otherwise the room reflects the Swedish imperial period, with wall decorations similar to Läckö Castle and Sandemar.

their wealth in industry and agriculture. The best example is the significant group known as "mountain men," who worked in the iron trade. The mountain mansions most closely associated with this self-assured group of entrepreneurs are found primarily in Västmanland, Närke, Dalarna, and Värmland.

One of the more famous "mountain mansions" is Sveden, near the Dalarna copper mines. The only remaining building is the so-called Wedding Cottage, where Carl Linnaeus celebrated his wedding on June 26, 1739. His bride, Sara-Lisa, was the daughter of the country doctor and town physician John Moraeus. Moraeus had redeemed his family estate in 1716, and it was presumably then that he erected his horizontal-timber "hall of happiness" with its double-room design.

The ceiling was originally covered with planks or overlapping split beams. An oil painting from 1819, by artist (and judge) Nils Asplund, depicts the original appearance of the house, which then consisted of three large timber wings enclosing a courtyard. One of the buildings is the Wedding Cottage. Unfortunately, the other two were demolished in the 1880s, when the present buildings were erected.

It is uncertain whether the preserved Wedding Cottage was built in the 1720s or 1730s, but the walls were probably decorated by Bernt Svedin, an artist from Dalarna who executed similar figural wall linen in other parts of Dalarna. He was active during the first half of the eighteenth century.

The vogue for using "Turkish" wall motifs in the decoration of reception and drawing rooms stems from the seventeenth century. Though called Turkish, these embellishments are not from Turkey. In fact, they are synonymous with Flemish wall coverings or tapestries, as they are now commonly known.

Daylight enters the reception hall through six leaded windows, giving an overall impression more associated with the seventeenth than the eighteenth century. The interior design is essentially the style that characterized the imperial period half a century earlier. This fashion spread among the affluent families of the bourgeoisie and the nobility, particularly in the timbered country houses erected in the middle of the eighteenth century. Though Sveden has never been a manor estate, that is, owned by the nobility, its owners—the mountain men—were allied with the aristocracy.

Above: Detail from Johan Henrik Scheffel's painting of Carl Linnaeus holding a linnaea flower.

Opposite: Detail of Linnaeus's collection cabinet at Hammarby.

Overleaf: The main building of Linnaeus's Hammarby, to the southeast of Uppsala, was completed in 1762.

The saddle roof of the Wedding Cottage was the most common roof of the period and afforded the possibility of furnished gable rooms in the attic. However, the main residence—which lay across the courtyard before it was demolished—had a two-level roof. This may be considered a manor roof, even though there are no window openings between the two roof levels.

The Wedding Cottage at Sveden is an important part of Sweden's cultural heritage, not only because it reflects the significance of the mountain men but also because it is a historical link to one of the country's most famous men. Moreover, the house has been spared rebuilding and modernization.

The furniture—mostly from the eighteenth century—bears witness to the so-called Vasa Renaissance and the Caroline baroque. The high-backed, leather-upholstered chairs in the main hall are presumably from the late 1730s. The tall cupboard is more traditional. Known commonly as "mountain men cupboards," such pieces, with an upper cupboard resting on small columns or pillars, were typical in Bergslagen. The oval table with baluster legs and robust edging appears to be from the early seventeenth century but could be from the early eighteenth century.

Monumental open fireplaces in the Wedding Cottage, built before the advent of the tile stove designed by Carl Johan Cronstedt in the 1760s, are intended to both light the room and radiate heat. Painted wood, rather than sandstone or limestone, was used for the mantelpiece. Molded cornices, which extend out around the open fireplaces, feature Corinthian acanthus leaves painted in trompe l'oeil.

Linnaeus's Hammarby

Carl Linnaeus purchased the Hammarby estate, in the parish of Danmark just outside Uppsala, in 1758. Four years later, the new building complex was complete. It consists of a main two-story building, made of dovetailed timber with a mansard roof, and two single-story wings. Linnaeus lived here with his wife and children until his death in 1778. He also had a house in Uppsala, a stone building adjacent to the Linnaeus Garden.

Like Råshult, Hammarby is a place of pilgrimage for Linnaeus enthusiasts. Owned by the state since 1879, the estate is also appreciated for its well-preserved eighteenth-century atmosphere. The interior

Above: Linnaeus's children were painted in a series of pastels, now hanging in the study at Hammarby.

Opposite: Carl Linnaeus's writing desk in his study. The walls are papered with botanical illustrations.

layout is similar to a double-room house, but the width of the building allows for more rooms. The reception room on the bottom floor is reminiscent of Sveden's Wedding Cottage, with its pairs of leaded windows. There is plain wood flooring throughout, made of wide pine or spruce floorboards with visible nail heads. The ceilings, made of planed planks, were originally whitewashed, though this treatment was removed at the end of the nineteenth century.

Linnaeus's widow, Sara-Lisa, inhabited Hammarby until her death; at that time, the estate passed to master horseman Ridderbjelke. Since its purchase by the state, the house and the surrounding parkland have been transformed into a museum. An extra story atop the east wing, which was added while the Linnaeus family still owned and lived at Hammarby, was removed. A turf roof was laid, and the building was restored to its original condition. Some of the furniture, mainly from the ground floor, was probably dispersed or discarded by Linnaeus's descendants. Some of the kitchen shelving has disappeared, though traces of it can be discerned on the sooty, exposed timber walls. The eighteenth-century open hearth, however, remains in place.

Linnaeus's study on the upper floor remains intact with its paintings, furniture, and tall leaded windows. The study windows, which face south and west, provide atmosphere for the whole house. Botanical wall charts pasted to the walls above the gray skirting board lend the room a unique flavor. The overall impression is late baroque. Some of the furniture was probably acquired before the house was built.

The bedroom, with its four-poster bed, is situated behind the study. Contemporary convention among the gentry stipulated separate suites for husband and wife, but the suite on the opposite side of the house seems to have been used as two drawing rooms rather than as drawing room and bedroom. The contemporary chairs in the drawing rooms may be the original rococo chairs taken from the dining room.

The embellishments of the outer drawing room are more elegant than those of the other rooms. The dado has floral decorations, and the original sheets of wallpaper, printed by Jon Uppström in Stockholm and

Above: The museum at Hammarby, designed to store Linnaeus's noted natural-history collection, is situated on a slope in the park behind the main building.

Opposite: The museum interior with Linnaeus's lecture pulpit, or "swotter," and collection cabinet.

Overleaf: A ground-floor room with distempered walls and leaded windows at Hammarby.

featuring a black-and-white floral pattern on a yellow background, still cover the walls. It may appear simple today, but it is important to remember that at the time the royal couple had the same style of printed wallpaper in their country residence at Svartsjö by Lake Mälaren.

A small museum is located on a slope behind the main building. A yellow, plastered brick building, the museum was erected in 1769 to house Linnaeus's famous natural-history collection. This collection is now kept at the Linnaeus Society in London, but the furniture, including a large collection cabinet, is still at Hammarby and contributes greatly to the eighteenth-century milieu. Also remaining at Hammarby are the books that belonged to Linnaeus, his lecture pulpit—"the swotter"—and his pupils' desks. The simple museum building, with its pyramidal tentlike roof, seems larger and more airy from the inside. The plain wood floor, the barred, vaulted windows, and the plain or painted furniture display the eighteenth-century interior at its best—simple, beautiful, and functional. The museum cabinets with rococo legs and doors, painted red on the inside, mix Swedish and Oriental influences. The repainted "swotter" with its adjustable armrest is not upholstered, in contrast to similar eighteenth-century chairs.

Hammarby estate testifies to a standard of construction and furnishing which was somewhat elevated above its station. It displays, on the one hand, elegance of an international stature. But on the other hand, its accessories betray more simple and primitive conditions, such as interior walls of exposed timber and a turf roof on the east wing. The mansard roof and red-oxide-painted timbers of the main building were still unusual when the estate was built. The surviving impression of Linnaeus's Hammarby is one of a large farmhouse rather than a country estate. But it is more than likely that in the eighteenth century the opposite was true: farmhouses of this size were not built until half a century later.

Fröreda

Red-oxide paint did not become common on large rural houses until the second half of the nineteenth century. Fröreda Storegård in the region of Småland is an exception to this rule. Fröreda originally consisted of several long, narrow, two-story buildings made up of two detached houses under a single roof. Only one of these double buildings retains its eighteenth-century guise. In several houses, some of the interior walls still have a late-baroque combination of wallpaper and elegantly painted areas on "mackle paper," similar to those at Hammarby and other upper-class

Opposite: A double building under one roof at Fröreda Storegård, from the second half of the eighteenth century.

Above: An interior from the upper story at Fröreda Storegård, with printed wallpaper featuring a late-baroque pattern from the mid-1700s. The built-in bed is painted with the same lamp-black gray as the paneling.

Opposite: Pasted wallpaper with hand-painted Gustavian-style floral decoration at Fröreda.

residences. There were no rolls of wallpaper in the eighteenth century; instead paper was pasted up sheet by sheet and then painted.

This eighteenth-century artistic treatment was to some extent commonly available, although decorated walls did not have a wider appeal until the nineteenth century. The printed, hand-painted wallpaper at Fröreda Storegård would have been just as fitting in a royal or noble country residence. The size and number of the rooms at Fröreda are, however, typically rural. The buildings and furnishings belong to the Gustavian period of 1770–80. The Gustavian style was first propagated during the period of Gustav III but was foreshadowed during the reign of his father, Adolf Frederik (1751–71). The changes were considerable—from dark, heavy, late baroque to light and airy rococo in the French style.

Strömserum

Numerous large country houses were built in both wood and stone during the 1760s and 1770s. One such house is Strömserum in Småland, a horizontal-timber construction. The main building is a significant example of the skills of a master timber builder. Only one of the original wings remains intact; the other burned down in the twentieth century. The remaining wing has proportions of such magnificence that it could easily serve as the *corps de logi* (main building) for a noble estate anywhere in the country.

A Deeply Rooted Tradition

The risk of fire was one of the greatest hazards in both town and country in the eighteenth century. The state's attempts to encourage building in stone stemmed not only from concerns over fire safety but also from stone's great symbolic value (partly due to its durability and partly due to its international status). Despite good intentions, the authorities' campaign was only partially successful. In Landskrona, for example, the state offered to give anyone who wished to build a house of stone—to designs by Carl Hårleman—both building stone and lime. Nonetheless, only a few dozen stone houses were built there during the eighteenth century. People in

Opposite: The impressive gable at Strömserum mansion in Småland, with its hipped mansard roof, was erected in the 1760s and 1770s.

Previous pages: Besides the impressive main building of Strömserum mansion, the estate originally had two large wings, though one burned in the twentieth century. The courtyard terminates in two smaller pavilions, of which one was a privy.

Overleaf: The long two-story garden facade of Strömserum mansion has rows of eleven windows—a translation into wood of rococo ideals from stone prototypes.

Sweden were simply used to building with wood; and besides, horizontally timbered houses did not have the problems with cold and damp that were associated with houses built of stone. Houses continued therefore to be built in wood but incorporated stone as a decorative element.

The detached or semidetached house is the primary symbol of building traditions from the sixteenth century on, but the six-room design with a central drawing room or salon is a result of eighteenth-century propaganda for better housing. The country house tradition, which was to have its breakthrough in the eighteenth century, is rooted in seventeenth-century building conditions.

Externally, the shape of the roof was the defining characteristic of houses for the upper-class or gentry. The typical shape was a two-part manor roof, either a hipped roof or one with timbering up to the roof ridge. After the mid-1700s, however, the mansard roof came to dominate in Sweden.

Näs

Näs, in the parish of Rö in Uppland, is an eighteenth-century horizontal-timber country mansion consisting of a main building and two single-story wings. The main building is clad with smooth paneling to resemble a stone house. It has a mansard roof, of which only the upper part is hipped. Näs was constructed between 1773 and 1775.

The front facade features a triangular gable with a window to light the attic story. There is an attic room, with windows right under the upper slope of the roof, at each end of the house. The six tall, large-paned windows reinforce the late-eighteenth-century impression. A fashion for such windows, derived initially from France, was prevalent when this house was built. It was not until the mid-nineteenth century, however, that such windows became widespread on rural houses. The lower, steeper part of the mansard roof is tiled, while the shallower upper section is covered with metal sheeting. Both materials served to diminish the risk of fire.

The much more risky method of laying roofs with tarred shingles was still used, as is evident on the wings at Näs. The exact age of these buildings is unknown, but they were most likely erected between 1730 and 1770. Both the upper and lower sections of the roofs are hipped; the design recalls a manor roof,

Above: Näs mansion in the parish of Rö in Uppland. The two single-story wings are timber structures with vertical paneling and tarred-shingle roofs.

Opposite: Detail of Näs mansion.

Overleaf: The billiard pavilion at Näs mansion was moved from its position near the main building into the park.

but there are no window openings between the two roof slopes. The outside walls are paneled, like those of the main building, and oil-painted in light gray. The windows are lower, almost square, and have outer shutters. The attic story was originally unfurnished. Elevated wall sections have inset windows to allow daylight to enter.

Näs is one of the most admired of the smaller eighteenth-century country mansions, not only for the exteriors of its main building and wings but also for its interiors. The tile stove and its piping system, invented by Carl Johan Cronstedt in collaboration with Fabian Wrede, was introduced in 1767. This improvement in heating fundamentally transformed Swedish living conditions, making it possible to inhabit more rooms during the winter months. It was therefore natural that all the rooms at Näs were equipped with cylindrical or straight tile stoves, elaborately decorated. Produced by the most skillful craftsmen in Stockholm, they were known as porcelain tile stoves. In the eighteenth century, the tile stove had a basic white glaze, which could be decorated with different colors. The stoves at Näs were installed on wooden rococo-style bases.

The walls were covered with woven linen treated with a mixture of calcium, glue, and water. The linen-covered sections were reduced in later years, but strips next to the tile stoves reveal the original wall decoration. The entrance hall is particularly well-preserved. Lintels over the gray-painted single doors are intact. Painted to resemble stone, the lintels were decorated with mottoes and crowned with antique cinerary urns. Such motifs were used in the eighteenth century as decoration and also as a reminder of transience and death.

The so-called billiard wing at Näs surely impressed the visitor. It is a separate pavilion that was used for billiards and other recreations. The room is rectangular, with six windows facing in three directions. The tall windows and doors and flourishing decorations are a manifestation of Gustavian elegance. The ceiling is

Above: Gatehouse at Misterhult in Småland.

Opposite: A picturesque place for contemplation in the park at Näs, this "gothic" tower was built in the early 1800s.

Overleaf: Skärva mansion near Karlskrona in Blekinge, a cross between peasant cottage, Roman pantheon, and Greek temple, is one of Sweden's more eccentric eighteenth-century creations. The house was built for shipbuilder Fredric Henric af Chapman.

whitewashed, with a molded cornice. The walls and windows are underpinned by a light gray dado, placed at the same height as the windowsills. Large-paned windows seem to invite the surrounding nature into the room. In this period, around the turn of the nineteenth century, a utilitarian view of nature had begun to transform into a passion for nature, suffused with almost religious overtones.

One of the buildings at Näs recalls this new appreciation for nature. It is a three-story wooden tower, almost gothic (in a literary rather than an architectural sense) in character. The two lower floors are ordinary rooms, while the third floor, reached by a bridge, is open to the air, covered only by a wooden roof.

Misterhult

An arrangement of enclosed groups of buildings flanking a courtyard was the rule in Sweden until the late 1700s. Main building, wings, and pavilions were connected by high fences, which had one or several gates, sometimes in the form of a small building. An example of this kind of "gatehouse" still stands at the Misterhult estate, on the coast of Småland, on the road passing beside the west wing of the courtyard. The wooden gatehouse, with its obelisk-like roof, was probably built in the 1770s and is a mixture of rococo and neoclassical elements. Such gatehouses were popular as an alternative to the ubiquitous baroque at the end of the seventeenth century.

Pleasure Houses and Pavilions

The modern form of the *lusthus* (pleasure house) was introduced during the seventeenth century, but its inspiration was classical. Magnus Gabriel De la Gardie built pleasure houses at several of his palaces, including Jacobsdal, Karlberg, and Läckö. They could take the form of a miniature ancient temple with columns or a round, square, or octagonal cupola-covered room. The pleasure house at Läckö Castle served almost as a summer residence for the count and his wife: they had separate suites joined by a porch.

A painted cupola from one of De la Gardie's seventeenth-century pavilions can still be found at the Ekholmen estate in Uppland. But most of the surviving pleasure houses and pavilions are from the eighteenth century.

Stora Nyckelviken

Stora Nyckelviken in Nacka was one of the country residences in the Stockholm area that attracted the most attention during the eighteenth century. It was leased as a summer retreat to the French ambassador. Both the rather modest, horizontal-timber main build-

Opposite: The pleasure house at Stora Nyckelviken in Nacka, outside Stockholm, reflects a passion for nature and Chinese culture. The small-paned windows are typical of the rococo period in Sweden.

ing, covered with oil-painted paneling, and the rectangular pavilion or billiard wing remain almost untouched since the rococo period. A two-story pleasure house stands on a rise west of the main building. This yellow-painted octagonal wood pavilion has a slightly sloping roof that can be used as a deck around the upper story. It is crowned by a high, bell-shaped roof with a weathervane. The color scheme is typical of the period—yellow walls with white window frames and moldings.

Medevi Spa

Few eighteenth-century buildings now serve their original functions. But there are exceptions, such as Medevi Spa in the province of Östergötland near Lake Vättern, which is still used as a spa. Its eighteenth-century dining room continues to serve guests, both those wishing to eat and those who have come to "take the water."

The red-oxide-painted, horizontally timbered building originated in the mid-1700s and was paneled and extended thereafter. Despite certain renovations, the interior appears more or less the same as it did during the time of the von Fersen family, who owned the spa during the second half of the eighteenth century. The large hall has tall windows and an impressive open fireplace. The vertical paneling is marbleized and complemented with painted pilasters.

Toward the end of the eighteenth century, architecture and furnishing liberated themselves from the strong influence of Carl Hårleman's rococo-inherited design. He and his peers were firmly based in functional thinking. Sparse elegance and woodworking traditions with French roots typified their buildings. During the 1780s, however, a "large style" was developed, with characteristics from Greco-Roman temple architecture, even though the material used was wood.

Svartå Ironworks and Foundry

Since Finland belonged to Sweden during the eighteenth century, buildings across the Baltic contribute to the country's architectural history. At Svartå, between Åbo (later known as Turku) and Helsinki, an impressive main building of horizontal timbers was built at the iron foundry to designs by Stockholm architect Erik Palmstedt.

The house had a mansard roof and was, at its highest, three stories. The external paneling was divided by pilasters lacking a base or capital (often used as "corner boxes") but with robust, Doric moldings above. Due to its size, the building has often been

Above: The dining room at Medevi Spa in Östergötland resembles an antique temple, while the exterior consists of paneled timber painted with red oxide.

Opposite: Detail of the base of a fluted Corinthian pilaster painted directly on planed planks at Medevi Spa.

Above: Detail of the wall decoration with columns and guéridons in the dining room at Svartå estate in southern Finland.

Opposite: The main building at Svartå is a wooden palace from the late 1700s. It is built of horizontal timbers and embellished with vertical paneling and moldings to imitate stone. The house was designed by architect Erik Palmstedt and constructed by local carpenters and joiners.

Above: Detail of paper decoration pasted directly on the timber walls of the upper staircase at Svartå estate.

Opposite: Large-paned windows were introduced in the last decades of the eighteenth century and came to be standard in nineteenth-century houses.

termed a "palace." Svartå's wood palace is one of the most impressive of its kind. The foundry owner's apartment is on the second floor. It is higher than the bottom story, which is evident on the exterior from the tall, large-paned windows.

The stately surroundings are even more marked in the interior: the Doric-inspired dining room features gray pillars on blue walls with faux medallions. The high, crested doors enhance the impression of an antique temple. But as in a theater, these are just props. The Gustavian-furnished apartment has timber walls, covered with woven linen or painted paper. It is illusionist art of the highest order.

Even if master builders and foundry owners constructed their "palaces" in wood, the interior ornamentation was state-of-the-art for Europe. Some of the rooms were fitted with decorated tile stoves from the Marieberg factory in Stockholm. Marieberg's faience products were characterized by a particularly lustrous glaze on yellow clay and seem to have been favored by the businessmen of the time. Rörstrand stoves, with their blue-and-white glazed-terra-cotta tiles, dominated the royal palaces. Provincially made stoves were installed in the Cavalier wing at Gripsholm Palace and at Ekolsund Palace, given to Gustav III while he was crown prince.

During the eighteenth century, Gustav III commissioned an inn that is still situated to the north of one of the wings at Ekolsund, on the old highway between Stockholm and Enköping. This building, privately financed by Gustav III, was a timbered house; its interior walls were plastered with a mixture of clay and organic material. It is not at all the stone building that Carl Fredrik Adelcrantz had planned for the king. It was not only Sweden's subjects who could not afford stone houses; economic reasons forced even the reigning monarch to build in wood.

Gunnebo

Merchant John Hall the elder was one of eighteenth-century Sweden's richest men. His sawmills and iron foundries gave him an ample fortune and allowed for the construction of perhaps the most magnificent country estate of this period. Gunnebo is a palacelike wooden building just outside Göteborg. The Hall family spent the summer months there. Carl Wilhelm Carlberg—Göteborg's town architect and nephew of Johan Eberhard Carlberg (Stockholm's town architect

Opposite: The main building of Gunnebo, in Mölndal, outside Göteborg, is a tour de force of antique elements—columns, capitals, and joists—translated into wood.

Overleaf: The west gable of the main building at Gunnebo faces the garden.

during the first half of the eighteenth century)—helped Hall to create a Swedish version of the ideal Italian villa. Planning and construction took almost twenty years.

The costs for Gunnebo, counted in barrels of gold, were astronomical. It was not only the main building and its furnishing that were costly; the careful provisions for draining surface water and rainwater from the garden were also quite expensive. Carl Wilhelm Carlberg's commission was not limited to the buildings and gardens of Gunnebo. He made special designs for each tile stove, matching its color scheme to the surrounding decoration. In fact, the color schemes of the individual rooms established the decor throughout. The joinery and stuccowork are of highest international quality.

Carlberg also designed furniture to correspond with the character of each room. This led to an unparalleled variety. Every detail on the estate—fencing, urns, and the like—was executed in accordance with the architect's meticulous designs. Indeed, the designed furniture at Gunnebo, particularly some of the pieces made to suit special rooms, spawned a furniture tradition in west Sweden, usually known as Lindone, after a parish in the province.

Gunnebo, which is really a summer retreat—even in its model, the Italian villa—is today known as Gunnebo Palace. Carl Wilhelm Carlberg must have executed his prolonged assignment in close cooperation with his employer. Yet he also must have questioned building such an exclusive summer retreat during a period when poverty in Sweden was prevalent. Even in the most elegant rooms at Gunnebo, the gilding of large mirrors and furniture was not allowed. Most of Carlberg's designs for Gunnebo have survived. Numbering over a hundred, they constitute Sweden's best-preserved and -documented early architectural project.

The visitor to Gunnebo is initially struck by its architectural composition, prepared in detail by Carlberg after careful studies in Europe, mainly England and France. The classical style of Gunnebo was developed in the late 1700s, partly at the French Academy of Art and royal palaces in France, and partly at English country estates. Antiquity was the ideal, but antiquity adapted to a comfortable eighteenth-century lifestyle.

By the time of John Hall's death in 1802, an expensive orangery had been erected at Gunnebo, its rooms elegantly furnished for the pleasures of the gentle-

Opposite: Detail of the large salon at Gunnebo with one of the chairs specially designed for the room. The wall behind features one of many fluted Ionic pilasters; to the right is an original plaster sculpture by the Italian artist Gioacchino Frulli.

Above: View from the large drawing room at Gunnebo into Mrs. Hall's antechamber.

Opposite: This serving table, like the other furniture at Gunnebo, was designed by architect Carl Wilhelm Carlberg.

folk. However, Hall's trading company went into liquidation, and his son, John Hall the younger, was never able to enjoy his inheritance.

The wings and the orangery have either burned down or been demolished, and the furniture has been scattered. It was not until the twentieth century that the hunt began for Gunnebo's original furnishings. Thanks to Carl Wilhelm Carlberg's designs, some of the original furniture has been identified. Mölndal's council purchased Gunnebo in the mid-1950s and began to reproduce furniture according to Carlberg's designs. Some of the original objects have also been restored. The goal to track down every piece of furniture and all the embellishments made for Gunnebo is slowly showing results.

Carlberg's detailed designs have also made it possible to re-create buildings that have disappeared, or to construct edifices that were planned but never realized (including a building for the servants and a henhouse). During the 1990s, the European Union subsidized a project to recover old building methods, in regard to both theory and practice. This project has given modern professionals a chance to familiarize themselves with craft skills that had almost disappeared.

Current rebuilding plans at Gunnebo include the wings, one of which contained a stable and coach house. The orangery is another likely element in the long-term renovation; today, however, only the foundations of the structure exist.

The Visionary Architect of Haga Park

There are a number of buildings in the Haga Palace area in Solna (or Haga Park, as it is known in the Stockholm area), and among them is Gustav III's pavilion—one of the few stone houses from the turn of the nineteenth century that would be a primary influence on the style of wood houses in the following century. It was erected during the 1780s but was not yet furnished when the king was murdered in 1792. The pavilion functioned as the royal couple's living quarters and continued to do so for the next generation, during the reign of Gustav IV Adolf.

Gustav III had met the French architect Louis-Jean Desprez in Rome during a visit to Italy. This meeting would change the history of Swedish architecture. The king wanted to appoint this visionary architect to an architectural position, but there were no free posts and so Desprez was employed as head of the opera's scenery department. The collaboration between the king and Desprez eventually led to a large-scale palace project, which was brought to a halt when Gustav III was murdered. Only the foundations were built.

Opposite: The "copper tent" at Haga Park in Solna was constructed to designs by Louis-Jean Desprez in about 1790. The building is made of wood but is covered with copper sheeting and painted to resemble a Turkish tent.

Louis-Jean Desprez had a pupil named Carl Christoffer Gjörwell who had designed the two wings of Karlberg Palace in the 1790s using Desprez's ideas. In 1802, the young king Gustav IV Adolf commissioned Gjörwell to design the building in Haga Park now known as Haga Palace. The structure was originally planned for Gustav IV Adolf's three children, two sons and a daughter. The sons' suites, with antechambers and bedrooms, were situated on either side of a large apartment that had three pairs of tall double doors. But the younger son died in 1803, before Haga Palace was fully furnished.

Corbels top each double door. The walls are painted in white-and-gray imitation marble. The robust stucco cornice emphasizes the official nature of the building. Each room was heated by a monochrome gray-white tile stove with moldings designed to imitate antique altars and columns. These classical motifs had already been introduced in Gustav III's nearby pavilion, but Haga Palace is more restrained and less decorated than the pavilion. Overall, this period is characterized by a penchant for stone (granite, porphyry, amber, and gray-white marble). Mahogany was the most popular wood, not just for furniture but also for interior doors and fixed mirror frames.

Haga Palace, or the royal children's building, came to be the standard for mansions, country houses, and villas. The middle section of the gable end extended a story higher than the rest of the two-story saddleback-roofed main building. This design recurs on many wood houses built during the first half of the nineteenth century in both Sweden and Finland. Unlike Gunnebo, Gjörwell's Haga has been imitated, undoubtedly since the more modest Haga was easier to translate into different variations than the magnificent and grandiose Gunnebo.

The saddle roof, with its shallower roof angle, though influenced by antique temples, had long been common in Sweden, especially on houses with turf roofs. The most severe form of the rectangular house with a two-level saddleback roof was introduced into Sweden by dilettante architect (and traveler in Italy) Carl August Ehrensvärd. He designed a utility building in Karlskrona in the province of Blekinge, the so-called inventory chamber.

Opposite: The dining room in Gustav III's pavilion in Haga Park was furnished during the late eighteenth century, but it foreshadows an aesthetic that came into its own at the beginning of the nineteenth century. The two serving tables resemble sarcophagus lids, as is typical of pieces in the empire style.

Nineteenth Century: Non-Aristocratic Mansion Builders

During the first years of the nineteenth century it became possible for commoners—those who were not aristocrats—to buy or procure mansions or manor houses. In this way, leading industrialists and businessmen became the most important mansion builders. Successful farmers, millers, and tradespeople also gained the means to build and buy manor houses.

Throughout the country remain impressive examples of buildings constructed by farmers during this period. This building activity bears witness to an increased self-confidence rather than a real need for housing. A boom in the building of timbered two-story buildings brought about the construction of almost as many aristocratic palaces as during the imperial period. As with structures for the nobility, the exterior was of primary importance. The farmers wanted to make a forceful impression. In the seventeenth century, the nobility often left attics unfurnished. This was also the case among the most successful farmers during the nineteenth century. In fact, it is said that farmers nailed the backs of chairs to windowsills on the upper story to give the impression that the rooms were furnished.

For successful businessmen, however, who had attained a high position in society through enterprise, there was a greater need to furnish the interiors throughout. The bourgeoisie was created and, with the increasing industrialization of the nineteenth century, came to form the leading strata of society, enjoying an entirely new level of economic resources.

Smelting House at Dylta Sulfurworks

During the nineteenth century, barrackslike workers' houses were built at ironworks and foundries and on estates. One such example is at Dylta sulfurworks in Närke. Instead of small, detached workers' residences, the typical housing was monumental, military-style barracks. At the turn of the twentieth century, such barracks were the most common new foundry buildings. The exteriors were often of high architectural quality, giving the district much prestige, even though the dwellings themselves were not particularly luxurious.

The smelting house, which housed eight families, consists of two attached buildings—which appear to

Opposite: Partial view of the south facade of the smelting house at Dylta sulfurworks in Närke. The lower story is stone and brick; the upper story is painted with a yellow wash.

Overleaf: The upper stories of the smelting house at Dylta sulfurworks have paneled facades. This eight-family residence was built around 1800 and was originally painted with Dylta's own red-oxide paint. The house was later painted yellow.

be one—with two separate entrances. Approached via an avenue of trees, the building embodies a neoclassical aesthetic. The bottom story is made of stone and brick, the second story consists of horizontal timbers, and the attic is half-timbered (wooden frame filled with stone or clay). The front and one side of the house are plastered; the upper stories on the rear of the building are paneled in wood. The paneling is painted with a yellow wash, which in the nineteenth century was the most distinguished treatment. Seventeenth-century mansions had red-oxide-painted horizontal timbers, but during the eighteenth century paneling and yellow paint became more common. This combination reached its peak during the nineteenth century, when it was used on both palace and shack.

The bottom story was built during the first years of the nineteenth century and features a double reversed six-room design. The impressive attic story has windows along its sides as well as a window high on the east gable.

The workers' quarters—which contained not only apartments with a kitchen but also two bakeries—probably were higher in status than the red-oxide-painted row, called the Ark, on the other side of the avenue of trees.

The question of why the owners of Dylta and similar foundries built such large, eye-catching housing for their workers at the end of the 1800s is pertinent, particularly in a comparison between the workers' barracks and the mansions of these foundries. The mansion house at Dylta was a relatively small, horizontal-timber building with a seventeenth-century ground floor; by 1800, a second story had been added. In contrast, the gable end of the smelting house—visible from quite a distance away—was painted yellow and given rows of blind windows. This treatment satisfied aesthetic needs but also gave the building monumentality. And in the wake of the French Revolution, the foundry owners may have wished to display some kind of political conscience.

Johannesberg

Johan Nyberg was an industrialist who had enjoyed a successful career in Ångermanland's timber industry. By the 1840s, he had founded numerous sawmills and procured a fleet of ships to transport building materi-

Above: Johannesberg in Bollstabruk, Ångermanland.

Opposite: The simple forms of classicism inspired the design of chairs in the early 1800s.

Overleaf: The kitchen and bedroom in one of the workers' lodgings at the Dylta smelting house. The timber walls on the upper story have been plastered with limestone and clay; originally, they were painted with lampblack up to the windowsill level.

Above: A window in one of the corridors on the upper story of the smelting house at Dylta sulfurworks.

Opposite: Chimney flues from the different lodgings at the Dylta smelting house merge in the attic before going up to the roof.

als from the Ångermanland coast to subcontractors in Europe, Asia, and America. From his profits, he built his own mansion, Johannesburg, in Bollstabruk. The two-story main building was probably constructed in 1842. The exterior is paneled and painted gray. The ground-floor paneling was designed to resemble stone, while the second story has vertical panels.

The front facade has nine windows and a pediment centered over the entrance. A semicircular, or "half-moon," window lights the attic. The building has a low saddle roof in the austere neoclassical, or empire, style. The mock stone is complemented with Gustavian ornamentation—bay-leaf garlands and rosettes carved in a style that carpenter Per Westman learned in Stockholm. Such ornamentation can be found both at the port city of Härnösand and in the surrounding parishes. The fan pattern above the entrance doorway reflects the more austere empire style. The type of wood carving that appears at Johannesberg was common on gilded mirror frames during the early 1800s. Sculpted anchors hang on each side of the door, symbolizing the owner's occupation.

The suite of rooms on the second floor surpasses most contemporary interiors in Stockholm. The great drawing room, or salon, has four windows facing the river below. Its walls are decorated above the dado with paintings depicting towns—among them Stockholm and Venice—and landscapes. The ceiling and cornices are richly ornamented. The remaining rooms on the second floor were decorated with imported wallpaper, ornamental painting, and modern furniture such as gilded mirror frames and mahogany chairs.

Bratteberg

Bratteberg, an inn in the parish of Regna in north Östergötland, has two wings from the 1850s and a porch from the early 1900s. The wings have pediments on each facade featuring lunette windows; this pattern was adopted from mansion architecture. The facade windows have fanned mullions, which are repeated in quarter-circle blind windows on the gable ends. These window frames are nailed to the black-

Above: Detail of the inn at Bratteberg in the parish of Regna, Östergötland. A timber wall has been pasted over with pages from old newspapers and books.

Opposite: During the 1850s, when the wings at Bratteberg were built, it was customary to paint the lower part of interior walls with a plain color or to marbleize them. Colorful wallpaper was pasted on the upper walls.

Overleaf: The gable of the south wing at Bratteberg. When the house was built the plain timber facades were not paneled. The design of the windows echoes Gustavian classicism and demonstrates a living timber-construction tradition.

painted timber, giving the impression of real window openings behind glass. One of the wings at Bratteberg served as a hardware store; the other was the hotel owner's residence. The carefully smoothed timber facades were originally painted with red oxide; window frames were light gray and "box ends" covered the timber joints. In the early 1800s, these projecting ends were hidden and dressed with planks to imitate stone.

When modernization came to middle Sweden—which was characterized primarily by the addition of a second story—these box ends were often painted with red oxide on farm houses; at vicarages and mansions, they were painted yellow or white. Toward the end of the nineteenth century, more individualized color schemes began to arise. In certain districts, the added upper story gave rise to a new kind of building—a one-and-a-half-story house with a saddle roof and overhanging eaves. Characteristic of this new type was a frontispiece with two or three windows.

Gingerbread Work

A novel tradition of carpentry rose out of this meeting between rural architecture and the ever more advanced sawmill industry and became particularly prevalent in the Ångermanland coastal region. Here, numerous large horizontal-timber houses were paneled to imitate stone architecture as closely as possible.

In northern Sweden, from the 1850s onward, doorways and entrance porches were strongly emphasized. In middle Sweden, entrance porches with saddle roofs had been built during the seventeenth century, especially on the "mountain mansions." The taste for entrance porches spread throughout Sweden at the end of the nineteenth century. The most popular version had a three-sided roof and fretwork ornamentation, usually known as "gingerbread work."

Above: Two different styles of porch on a farmhouse at Alfta in the Hälsingland region. The porch on the left has a curved roof supported by two corner pillars; the porch on the right has a pediment with a fretwork fringe.

Opposite: The Gustavian interest in classical forms during the early 1800s flourished in north Sweden. This colorful and richly decorated porch was built in 1845 at Runemo, Alfta.

Overleaf: Matsgården in the village of Östbjörka in the region of Dalarna, now owned by the Nordic Museum, is typical of hundreds of years of enclosed Scandinavian farms. It was not until the 1800s, however, that farmhouses were built with two stories.

Above: Large living rooms, such as the one at Matsgården, were used for eating, working, and sleeping and were central in traditional Swedish farmhouses until the nineteenth century. The farmer's bed was often an imposing built-in feature placed in one corner, in this instance incorporating a grandfather clock.

Opposite: Different ages meet in the farmyard at Matsgården—unpainted timber stands alongside the box ends and red-oxide-painted facades fashionable in the nineteenth century.

Overleaf: The cow shed at Matsgården has an open fireplace and space for a bed. The roof is supported by heavy beams made of split logs.

Above: This residence in Holen outside Tällberg in Dalarna was built in the style of a Caroline mansion by painter and folklore researcher Gustaf Ankarcrona at the turn of the twentieth century. An interest in old construction skills, including the "mountain mansions," is reflected in the small-paned windows, shutters, and cross-jointed timber facades of the house.

Opposite: The nineteenth-century interest in antiquity saved Holen, and many other old buildings, for posterity.

Previous pages: Only a few old buildings used for small industry still stand, as does this one at Gimåfors in central Medelpad.

Overleaf: The invaluable remains of Sweden's ancient building tradition, whether in the form of single houses or whole farms and so strongly evident at Holen, are to a large extent the result of the work of artists and folklore researchers, such as Gustaf Ankarcrona and Anders Zorn, active in Dalarna in the late 1800s.

Toward a New Age

In 1868, an important book containing designs for wooden houses was published. Though titled *Rural Buildings, Mainly for Smaller Farms*, it came to be influential for the design of railway communities and new industrial areas. Many of the designs, by Charles Emil Löfvenskjöld, feature the six-room layout, used in numerous larger rural houses built during the late 1800s.

Löfvenskjöld, an architect interested in practical matters, even designed outhouses for farms. He has sometimes been called "the barn architect," an epithet that reflects the low regard in which this type of building was held—such utilitarian buildings were typically not of interest to architects.

Nevertheless, Löfvenskjöld's impact on Swedish wood architecture can be seen throughout the country. His buildings are characterized by traditional horizontal-timber framework and designs from the eighteenth century adapted to single-story houses and furnished attics. The exterior design was more modern, featuring porches, roof trusses, and gable ends with ornamental fretwork. In contrast to empire-style architecture, Löfvenskjöld concentrated on the inherent qualities of wood as a material.

A new kind of villa architecture, often characterized by external stairs, asymmetrical facades, and towerlike features, appeared during the early twentieth century. Most typical of this period is a free relationship to tradition, influenced primarily by English ideas. Löfvenskjöld's designs, also published in *Teknisk tidskrift* (a professional magazine for building construction and techniques), could be used as a source of inspiration for builders and carpenters composing their own designs.

The construction of summerhouses began in earnest during the twentieth century. The transition from agricultural society to modern towns with railway connections brought about a change in architectural culture. Architects began to build in a way that was not directly limited to local, inherited tradition.

An interest in the Middle Ages arose in Germany during the mid-nineteenth century as architects began to design houses reminiscent of medieval castles. The phrase "Swiss style," which has been used in Sweden to describe houses with overhanging eaves and rich ornamentation, is in fact also characteristic of Löfvenskjöld's work, as are open or glass verandas framed with fretwork. The late nineteenth century was also the golden age of Orientalism. The so-called

Opposite: The Ribersborg bathing house, standing on wooden piles in the Øresund strait at Malmö, was constructed in the early 1900s. Certain features were borrowed from medieval castles.

Overleaf: An early-twentieth-century, national-romantic house facade, reflecting the fondness for imaginative latticework.

Turkish pavilion at Haga had been built in the eighteenth century, but in the nineteenth century Sweden was overrun with pleasure houses, bathing houses, and verandas ornamented with Oriental- and medieval-inspired motifs. Norwegian stave churches also contributed to the architectural mix. Sweden was strongly inspired by Norwegian wood architecture, partly due to the union (1814–1905) between Sweden and Norway. The founding of the Nordic Museum and Skansen, the world's first open-air museum, increased general interest in the shared Viking culture.

A prefabricated house, constructed at the Ekman workshops outside Stockholm, was sent to the 1876 Centennial Exhibition in Philadelphia. This building, which featured horizontal, loglike tarred paneling, today stands as the marionette theater in New York City's Central Park. At the Centennial Exhibition, the building was presented as a modern schoolhouse in medieval guise. The uses for such an industrially produced building were unlimited—it could serve as permanent residence, summerhouse, or school.

Historical inheritance was a rich source of inspiration at the turn of the twentieth century. Even leading architects borrowed heavily without fear of being labeled nostalgic. One of the most famous Swedish buildings in the "Viking style" is a villa at Lysekil, commissioned by cultural personality Dr. Carl Peter Curman during the 1870s. The building features tarred facades, projecting eaves, and galleries and represents a conscious attempt to create a new, national, historically inspired style. Also apparent in this house is an attempt to recover traditional skills and working methods.

By the turn of the century, the "Viking style" had become popular among educated and affluent Swedes. The villa community of Djursholm was founded at Stora Värtan, to the north of Stockholm. This group was developed in accordance with English ideas of living in harmony with nature. Viktor Rydberg's house is one example, illustrating contemporary fashions in both building and furnishing. Rydberg's study has subsequently been installed at the Nordic Museum.

Generally, after 1880 room layout was less formal. In classical tradition, austere symmetry had been almost obligatory, but with the new stylistic ideals, imaginative additions became far more common. The

Above: This blue bathing house, which resembles a classical temple, was built at Hasseludden, in Stockholm's archipelago, at the turn of the twentieth century.

Opposite: Despite the overhanging eaves and rich fretwork on this summerhouse at Kungsholmen in Stockholm, the structure represents Swedish eighteenth-century tradition and has a six-room layout inspired by Andrea Palladio.

Overleaf: Bathing houses at Pålsjöbaden in Hälsingborg stand like a small town on the water.

Above: Detail from an open veranda. A nineteenth-century interest in antiquity and exotic cultures inspired new forms in wood architecture.

Opposite: The rediscovery of Gustavian forms inspired early-twentieth-century architects and furniture designers to create light, sunny, white rooms with large-paned windows.

Overleaf: Beach huts on Fårö Island with tarred roofs and walls.

Above: The weathered wood of a fishing hut at Djupvik on Gotland.

Opposite: A row of fishing huts at Djupvik.

new love for asymmetry was displayed, for example, in L-shaped buildings, often with projecting turrets. Great pride was taken in surprise effects, symbolizing a liberation of the mind from the rule of order. In reaction to the stifling classical tradition arose an almost irrepressible desire for freedom of form.

Many ideas on architectural renewal came from England. *The Studio* (a magazine presenting new thinking about art, first published in 1893) was a source of inspiration for Karin and Carl Larsson, for instance, when they designed their own house at Sundborn. And English artist-philosopher John Ruskin, already active in the 1850s, found his best interpreters in Sweden at the turn of the twentieth century.

Ellen Key, a feminist writer who covered a wide variety of topics, including aesthetics, called for a high level of design for all classes of society, not just the wealthy. Her aesthetic, particularly attuned to light and space in the home, borrowed elements from the Gustavian period, as did Sundborn. Light-colored paneling and furniture, whitewashed ceilings, and large-paned windows provided a natural airiness. The Gustavian room was in stark contrast to the dark, draped, walnut-furnished room of the late nineteenth century. Light regained its place of honor in the early twentieth century. Simultaneously, a strong folklore movement developed, resulting in the formation of the Swedish Society of Crafts and Design. Local folklore and handcraft societies were founded to safeguard traditions and designs that were disappearing in modern industrial society.

Such nationalistic self-assertion could already be discerned, however, at the end of the previous century. After the dissolution of the union with Norway in 1905, many people began to search for a "pure" Swedish identity in contrast to the earlier Norwegian-Swedish one.

Carl Larsson was one of the most influential figures in the search for a new Swedish identity. His illustrations in books such as *Ett hem* (*A Home*, 1899), *Spadarfvet* (*Spade Inheritance*, 1906), and *Åt solsidan* (*On the Sunny Side*, 1910) have come to be a kind of national prototype for living in harmony with nature and the seasons. He drew inspiration from both the Gustavian period and old peasant society, from both the drawing room and the rustic cottage.

This lifestyle, as evidenced at the Larsson house, Sundborn, influenced the summerhouse ideal, as did the fusion of old and new. Even when functionalism was at its peak in the 1930s, austere eighteenth-century furniture appealed to the modern aesthetic. Plain Windsor chairs and tables with tapering legs and a minimum of decoration have become a timeless symbol of Sweden's furniture tradition.

Opposite: Fishing huts with paneled facades at Gnisvärd, Gotland.

Nordic Wood Churches

Throughout Scandinavia, the Catholic Middle Ages survive in the form of wood and stone churches. During the first century of Christianity in Sweden (tenth century), so-called stave churches—churches built of partially embedded vertical timbers—probably dominated. During the twelfth century, stone buildings gradually replaced these stave churches, also common in Norway. In this period the district of Bohuslän belonged to Norway, and it was there that King Olaf Tryggvason founded a stone church, at Svenneby beside Bottna Fjord, that survives today.

Of the Swedish stave churches, only one remains on its original site, at Hedared, Västergötland. Modest in appearance, the structure provides evidence of the Catholics' desire to build larger and more monumental buildings to represent their church. In Norway, however, more stave churches have survived—partly due to their remote locations and partly because the peasant population, in contrast to that in Sweden, maintained ownership of the parish land. Urnäs stave church stands as a living monument of the Viking era and is one of Scandinavia's most remarkable art treasures. The masterfully carved dragons that coil around the entrance porch are undamaged after a thousand years. The church building resembles a large, wide, clock tower; its upper walls and roof are covered with tarred-wood shingles. Romanesque sculptures and a Protestant altar, pulpit, and pews coexist under the high ceiling. The choir has retained its railing. In most other churches, from the seventeenth century on, these partitions were removed to create more space in the nave for large funerals.

Most of the medieval churches that have survived in Sweden are those built of stone. For example, Enånger Church, on the coast of Hälsingland south of Hudiksvall, and Ytterlännäs Church, by the Ångerman River, are veritable treasures. New, larger churches for the growing populations of those congregations were built on nearby sites. At the end of the nineteenth century, there were still considerable numbers of medieval churches in Sweden, but many of them have since been demolished. The Romanesque ashlar church at Hamneda in Småland met such a fate; it was destroyed with dynamite at the turn of the twentieth century.

The practice during the nineteenth century of reusing building materials from older churches had no

Opposite: Detail from the twelfth-century entrance porch at Urnäs stave church in Norway. Tar has preserved the sinuous Viking decoration.

Overleaf: Urnäs stave church is located on an ancient meeting place between steep mountains and the deep Sogne Fjord. The vertically timbered walls support a high, steep, tarred-shingle roof.

Above: An expressive thirteenth-century Romanesque wood sculpture at Urnäs stave church.

Opposite: A Protestant altar presides over the choir of Urnäs. The choir doors partition off the main church.

basis in spiritual symbolism but instead reflected practical economic concerns. However, the parishioners at Ytterlännäs and Enånger succeeded in saving their old churches. Closed for some time, the sanctuaries have now been brought back into use, especially during the summer.

The destruction of medieval sculptures or wall paintings was not done to obliterate Catholic symbols but rather for aesthetic reasons. Medieval paintings were often whitewashed during the 1700s, for example, when a window was enlarged or a vault repaired. It is remarkable to see the remaining late-medieval altar sculptures, such as those in Ytterlännäs Church, which include an early-sixteenth-century altarpiece of the Virgin and child. Catholic symbols exist alongside the Protestant paintings on the pulpit gallery, demonstrating that the Reformation was mostly administrative, reflected more in the language of the service than in church decoration.

In this context, it is important to recall an event that affected not only Sweden but the whole of Scandinavia. On the night of November 12, 2001, a well-preserved medieval wood building, the horizontal-timber church at Södra Råda, in southern Värmland, burned to the ground. Probably the finest suite of fourteenth- and fifteenth-century paintings in Scandinavia perished. Södra Råda Church must now serve as a memorial to the vulnerability of such cultural treasures.

It is a mystery how rich artistic ornamentation and decoration in churches, castles, and mansions could have been accomplished during the first half of the eighteenth century. These were hard times in Sweden, particularly the first decades, but decorative painting flourished as never before. Though Sweden had attained an important position in Europe during the seventeenth century, the imperial period was now just a memory. Presumably there was an even greater need to create monuments of important artistic content for posterity. The kind of decorative painting done at Läckö Castle in the 1670s, for example, could now be seen in numerous churches in that district.

The largest and most unusual of these early-eighteenth-century churches is at Habo parish, in

Above: In the 1850s, the medieval church at Ytterlännäs was replaced by a new parish church. The old church fell into disuse, thus saving the Renaissance and baroque decorations.

Opposite: Interior of the medieval church at Ytterlännäs. The double gallery and sculptured and painted corbels help make this one of Sweden's most authentic churches.

southeast Västergötland. Paintings with biblical references cover the walls, ceiling, and galleries. Strangely enough, this large horizontal-timber church was constructed during the most severe years of the Great Northern War, at the end of the 1710s, when a great part of the Swedish army was imprisoned in Siberia and plague and famine afflicted the country.

Habo and other timber churches poignantly demonstrate the long-term importance of artistic building and decorative painting. The wooden church at Bottnaryd, between Jönköping and Ulricehamn, is older and smaller than Habo Church. It was erected during the 1660s, but the timber walls and ceiling were not decorated until several decades later.

During the second half of the eighteenth century, many wooden churches were built in Finland (which then belonged to Sweden). There is a remarkably well-preserved timbered 1760s church at Petäjävesi, north of Helsinki. The bare timber walls of the porch have never been painted. The timbers were not cross-jointed, as was usual, but dovetailed. Timber craftsmen, using improbably simple tools, constructed Petäjävesi Church with remarkable skill. The building is a work of genius, especially for its strength.

The roots of Petäjävesi Church can be traced back to Katarina Church, a cruciform church on Södermalm in Stockholm designed by Jean de la Vallée in the 1650s. Numerous late-seventeenth-century horizontal-timber country churches were based on Katarina Church, such as Ramundeboda Church in Närke (now moved to Laxå).

Another example of a dovetailed timber building is Seglora Church in Västergötland, constructed in 1729–30. It was moved to Skansen in Stockholm in the 1910s. The exterior retains its original red-tarred shingles. In 1785–86, a timber-paneled tower was added to replace a separate clock tower. It features an octagonal pavilion-like crown with a cupola. Baroque influence is manifest, particularly in Västergötland. The shingled tower roofs on Läckö Castle—erected during Magnus Gabriel De la Gardie's time—have been copied in many church towers.

A pleasure house commissioned by De la Gardie, originally on an island in Eken archipelago outside Läckö, was moved during his lifetime to the newly founded town of Lidköping. It was reerected on the square where it still stands, though it was partly renovated in the twentieth century after a fire.

Opposite: This tower, clad in red-tarred shingles, was added to Seglora Church, in Västergötland, in the 1780s. The church was moved to Skansen in Stockholm in the 1910s.

Above: Petäjävesi's cruciform, galleried, timber church, built during the 1760s.

Opposite: One of the side doors at Petäjävesi has planed moldings, both for decoration and construction purposes.

Overleaf: The bottom story of the Petäjävesi clock tower is cruciform in plan to support the tower above.

Above: When Magnus Gabriel De la Gardie restored this medieval monastery church at Varnhem in Västergötland, he added a new, shingled central tower with a tall seventeenth-century baroque spire.

Opposite: Detached clock tower at Delsbo Church, built in 1741. Separate church towers were the rule until the eighteenth century, when towers began to be built atop the church itself.

Nordic Wood Towns

Until Norway was placed under the rule of Denmark with the Union of Kalmar at the end of the fourteenth century, Norwegian architecture followed its own distinct path. After 1397, Danish sovereignty extended its influence primarily to the architecture of Norwegian towns and iron foundries; rural dwellers continued to follow their own traditions. Even today horizontal-timber houses from the Middle Ages, mostly cabins on stilts or farmhouse attics, remain in Norway. In Bergen, one of the few towns where medieval wooden buildings have survived, stand Hansa-period wooden houses. With gable ends facing the street, they resemble houses in northern German towns, such as Lübeck, except that the buildings in Germany are brick or half-timbered. Norwegian houses are clinker-built (with overlapping, horizontal planks), in contrast to those in Sweden, where paneling is usually vertical.

Røros is another well-preserved town in Norway, with many cross-jointed timber one- or two-story houses, often without protective paneling. Røros has the character of a large village, with enclosed farmyards alongside the winding streets. Photographs from the 1860s indicate that Swedish towns, including larger towns such as Uppsala, were probably very similar, at least until the mid-nineteenth century. Significant areas of wooden housing survive in a few towns in Sweden, as in Vimmerby and Eksjö, and single houses or blocks have been preserved in a greater number of towns, including Karlskrona, Ronneby, and Karlshamn. Skottsberg, in Karlshamn, is a merchant's townhouse that is now owned by the Nordic Museum and is partially open to the public.

Finland was part of Sweden until the 1809 Russian annexation. Swedish-speaking districts along the Baltic coast and in Österbotten had enjoyed a lively trade with Sweden for at least a thousand years. Russian occupation caused great political change, but everyday life continued much as before. The Russian czar, Alexander I, confirmed Swedish as the official language in the autonomous duchy in Borgå in 1809.

Finland's separation from Sweden led to somewhat of a consolidation and strengthening of old traditions. At the same time, artistic impulses from the Russian capital at the time, St. Petersburg, flowed into the country. Prosperity increased and the wars that had plagued Finland, especially during the early eighteenth century, were a thing of the past. Finland regained its previous size when the Russians returned territory—from the region of Karelen as far as Ladoga—that Finland had lost during Karl XII's reign.

Stone buildings were unusual in Finland during the Swedish occupation, with the exception of

Opposite: Bergen, Norway, is one of the only towns where wooden houses from the Hansa period survive. Their horizontally paneled gable ends face the street.

Above: Wooden house facades in Bergen.

Opposite: Bergen house facades and roofs reflected in centuries-old windowpanes.

Overleaf: The Skottsberg house in Karlshamn is now a museum. It is an unusually well-preserved eighteenth-century ensemble, with a two-story, paneled, rococo main house on the street and outhouses enclosing the cobbled yard.

Above: The painted decorations in the drawing room of Skottsberg were influenced by contemporary Gustavian designs.

Opposite: The staircase to the upper story of Skottsberg is enclosed with imitation balusters.

Overleaf: Skottsberg's large dining room features late-Gustavian wall decorations and a decorated rococo tile stove on a wooden base.

medieval churches, fortifications such as Åbo and Tavastehus, and a few palaces, including Villnäs and Sarvlax. Finnish nobility built mansions primarily in timber. During the eighteenth century, however, some foundry mansions were constructed in stone, such as at Fagervik in southern Finland. Svartå, on the other hand, boasts an excellent example of a large, timber foundry mansion. Towns in Finland were almost entirely built in wood—usually one-story houses with yellow-painted paneling—until the twentieth century. A few stone houses in Åbo (later known as Turku) and Helsinki are an exception to the rule.

The center of Åbo, Finland's second-largest city, was preserved until the 1950s. It consisted of wooden one- and two-story houses built after a devastating fire in 1827, which also destroyed the cathedral and newly built university building. As a result of this fire, Helsinki was made capital of the Russian duchy. Architectural taste leaned toward the Russian empire style as well as designs by Finland's leading architect of the early 1800s, the German-born Carl Ludvig Engel. To his credit are a number of monumental buildings surrounding Nikolai Church in central Helsinki, including senate and university buildings at Senate Square. The Governor's Palace on the south of the square and the university library are also characterized by Engel's classicism, itself inspired by monumental buildings in St. Petersburg by Italian architect Giacamo Quarenghi.

Quarenghi had studied at the French Academy in Rome, as had Louis-Jean Desprez—architect of the unrealized palace at Haga. Desprez's favorite pupil, Carl Christoffer Gjörwell, had been commissioned by Gustav IV Adolf to build a new university building in Åbo in 1801.

Gjörwell's main building for Åbo Academy—as the university was known before the fire of 1827 and the move to Helsinki—came to be Sweden's largest and most expensive building project since Gustav III's reign. When Sweden lost Finland in 1809, the completion of Gjörwell's university building became the responsibility of Russia. After Gustav III was killed in 1792, his adviser Gustaf Mauritz Armfelt fell out of favor with Count Karl, the protector during Gustav IV Adolf's childhood. Armfelt was accused of treason and left the country, but his influence was renewed, particularly with Czar Alexander I, after the annexation of Finland. Armfelt

Above: The town of Røros in northern Norway resembles a group of closely built, horizontally timbered farms.

Opposite: Detail of facades in Røros.

Overleaf: During the nineteenth century, Finnish wooden towns such as Nådendal took their design inspiration from St. Petersburg. Both new and older houses were paneled and given different hues with oil paints.

subsequently commissioned Gjörwell to modernize his Finnish estate of Åminne. The mahogany and bronze-gilt furnishing made its library the most magnificent of its age, and the czar was so impressed that he copied the design for one of his own palaces.

After the fire of 1827, Åbo was rebuilt with one- and two-story houses in a homogeneous empire style. Rauma, another Finnish wooden town, was untouched by fire and thus displays a variety of antiquated styles. The public face of Rauma was also influenced to some extent by the Russian empire style, while the back streets and yards display a kind of vernacular architecture with yellow and red facades.

Toward the end of the nineteenth century, Finnish wood architecture developed a richness that is typically Russian. Timber walls are covered with horizontal paneling, and corbels appear above and below windows that are framed with Italian Renaissance decoration adapted to rustic materials.

The wooden facades were decorated with nature-inspired motifs that may be associated with Art Nouveau. Since this style of decoration is found in neither Norway nor Sweden, the inspiration presumably came from Germany and England. It is possible that Finland wished to assert its independence from Russia and therefore looked west, to English and German architects, for inspiration.

Though surface treatment differentiates their buildings, wooden architecture in Norway, Sweden, and Finland has an undeniable common origin in the so-called horizontal-timber tradition. Wood churches provide a common resource for "Nordic" wood building traditions in these three countries. Such churches display, on the one hand, an ancient medieval tradition from stave churches and, on the other, an assimilation of Protestant church design, both spatially and with regard to construction techniques. The Petäjävesi cruciform church in southern Finland is just one example.

In contrast to Europe's agricultural workers, members of Scandinavia's rural population, though heavily taxed by the so-called free men, were free to create their own culture. The result was a self-assured folk culture that left a lasting impression, particularly in churches. The serfdom dominant to the east and south of the Baltic is reflected architecturally by a lack of vernacular architectural expression. Even in the Polish region of Pomeranian, once part of the Swedish empire,

Above: Simple house facades in Rauma.

Opposite: Rauma provides rich examples of decoration, including horizontal paneling, boxing, and window framing with robust neo-Renaissance accents.

Overleaf: The backyards in Rauma are considerably plainer than the street facades.

the nobility dictated the appearance of churches. In Swedish, Norwegian, and Finnish country churches, however, the seventeenth- and eighteenth-century interiors are stamped with the popular taste.

Building culture in the districts of southern Sweden (which were Danish until the mid-seventeenth century) have more in common with Denmark and northern Germany than with the rest of the country. The lack of wood in this region gave rise to a long tradition of half-timbering. Moreover, in the late medieval period, the church wielded great power in the Danish parts of Sweden because of its extensive land holdings. At the time of the Reformation, church property was transferred to the king and state, and later given to the nobility, already owners of large estates. It was not until the eighteenth century that a folk culture, reminiscent of that in the north, developed in southern Sweden. The free farmers in the region of Skåne experienced prosperity during the nineteenth century and built mansionlike houses to demonstrate their new position.

Bricks had been used to build churches in Skåne as early as the late twelfth century. Half-timbering was almost totally replaced by brick during the second half of the nineteenth century but became fashionable again in the twentieth century. Northern parts of Skåne, however, always had extensive forested lands, and the wood houses in the district share many building traditions with southern Småland. The Danish inheritance lives on in the areas of Skåne, Halland, and Blekinge. The typically long and narrow houses are half-timbered, horizontally timbered, plastered, or brick.

Drakamölla farm in Österlen, which has been restored by art historians Ingemar and Britt Thunander, is one of the treasures of the half-timber building tradition. Society in Österlen, which was not integrated with Sweden until after the Danish wars of the 1670s, was more feudal than elsewhere. Large estates dominated, and it was only at the end of the eighteenth century that self-ownership among farmers started to develop. The real breakthrough for self-ownership came in the mid-1800s, after comprehensive distribution reforms. Twentieth-century town architecture in Skåne also had Danish prototypes, particularly evident in its many railway communities.

Opposite: Yellow-painted facades with red window framing in Sveaborg.

Overleaf: The silent forests of Sweden, which once provided building material for much of the country, are still the heart of the land.

First published in the United States of America in 2003 by
The Monacelli Press, Inc., 902 Broadway, New York, New York 10010.

First published in 2002 by Bokförlaget Prisma, Sweden, as *Svenska Trähus*
Published by agreement with the Pan Agency

Copyright © 2002 Ingalill Snitt (photographs) and Lars Sjöberg (text)
English edition © 2003 The Monacelli Press, Inc., and Bokförlaget Prisma

All rights reserved under International and Pan-American Copyright
Conventions. No part of this book may be reproduced or
utilized in any form or by any means, electronic or mechanical,
including photocopying, recording, or by any information storage and
retrieval system, without permission in writing from the publisher.
Inquiries should be sent to The Monacelli Press, Inc.

Library of Congress Cataloging-in-Publication Data
Sjöberg, Lars, date.
The Swedish house / photography by Ingalill Snitt ; text by Lars Sjöberg.
p. cm.
ISBN 1-58093-129-4
1. Architecture, Domestic—Sweden. I. Snitt, Ingalill. II. Title.
NA7382.S56 2003
728'.37'09485—dc21   2003012354

Translated from the Swedish by Martin Heap
Printed and bound in Italy